WHY VENEZUELA?

HOW THE US TRIES TO UNDERMINE DEMOCRACY
AND SOVEREIGNTY IN LATIN AMERICA

1804
books

Print edition published in September 2025 by
1804 Books, New York, NY

1804Books.com

ISBN: 979-8-9990195-2-3

Previously published in Spetember 2024 as an electronic edition.

Edited by Zoe Alexandra
Cover by Vivek Venkatraman

TABLE OF CONTENTS

INTRODUCTION
WHY WE STAND WITH VENEZUELA

BY MANOLO DE LOS SANTOS

For over a century, the United States has aggressively pursued global dominance, intensifying its efforts in recent years to maintain its role as unipolar power and world policeman. Billions are funneled into wars as the US seeks to consolidate its control and punish dissenting voices that resist its dictated world order. While major power conflict with Russia and China has been at the forefront of its foreign policy in recent times, the United States has sought to undermine the independence and sovereignty of Cuba since 1959 and of Venezuela since 1999, attacking both with a unique obsession and severity.

Venezuela has emerged as a significant focal point of struggle against US imperialism in the twenty-first century. For this, Venezuela has faced crippling US economic sanctions since 2005, a tactic aimed at subjugating nations that resist US hegemony. Ostensibly aimed at punishing a "corrupt government," the true motives are clear: to gain control over Venezuela's vast natural resources and to crush a center of revolutionary transformations in Latin America. This leads us to the question: Why Venezuela?

To understand this, we must recognize that the events of the past twenty-five years represent a genuine revolution. Millions of working-class Venezuelans, particularly women, Black, and Indigenous people, have fought to reclaim power from the elite, reshaping the state to fulfill their collective aspirations. They have rewritten the constitution to reflect their realities and reclaimed their natural resources for massive wealth redistribution, providing health care to millions and constructing over five million homes in the last decade alone.

Venezuela's revolution has also played a pivotal role in uniting countries across the continent, forming alliances like UNASUR (Union of South American Nations), CELAC (Community of Latin American and Caribbean States), and ALBA-TCP (Bolivarian Alliance for the Peoples of Our America—People's Trade Treaty) to counter US influence in the region. Venezuela represents the greatest political threat to the US policy of the Monroe Doctrine, which positions the Caribbean and Latin America as an American "backyard," justifying exploitation and domination rather than respecting their sovereignty.

As Venezuela has constructed a base for Latin America's political and economic independence from US influence, the US has retaliated with a barrage of political, cultural, and media attacks, spreading disinformation. The Trump administration's deliberate efforts to destabilize the Venezuelan economy in 2017–2019, including imposing punishing sanctions, led to a staggering 90 percent drop in GDP and the seizure of billions of dollars in Venezuelan assets abroad.

These sanctions are not mere punitive measures—they are unilateral and coercive actions that devastate the daily lives of ordinary people. Reports indicate that over one hundred thousand Venezuelans have died due to lack of medicine and food. This has also triggered mass migration, reversing Venezuela's historical role as a safe haven for those fleeing violence in neighboring countries.

Amidst this turmoil, the Venezuelan people see Washington as the true antagonist, orchestrating suffering through its local proxies, but for them, the choice is clear: to uphold their sovereignty and dignity against US intervention. The stakes extend beyond political leadership; they represent a battle for the nation's survival against foreign interests that seek to privatize public resources and dismantle social programs.

The question remains: Will Venezuela chart its own destiny or allow the US to dictate its future? For millions, President Nicolás Maduro symbolizes a commitment to protecting their interests, standing firm against imperialist attacks.

Despite relentless external pressures, the unity of the Venezuelan people and their leadership has thwarted US efforts to destabilize the government. From failed coup attempts to mercenary invasions, the strategies employed have consistently underestimated the resolve of the Venezuelan masses.

This book amplifies bold voices from across the region, delving into the roots of the Bolivarian Revolution and its grassroots character. The essays critique the US and Venezuelan opposition's roles in undermining this revolution, exposing the media's distortions and the roots of the right wing in Venezuela.

Understanding Venezuela is crucial for working people everywhere, as it reveals the broader machinations of US imperialism in this critical moment. The scars from previous US-sponsored dictatorships remain fresh for many in Latin America, serving as a stark reminder of the cost of intervention. The fight for Venezuela is not just a struggle for national liberation—it resonates throughout the continent, illuminating the ongoing battle for sovereignty, dignity, and social justice against imperialist forces.

EDITOR'S NOTE

On January 10, 2025, the US State Department announced that it was increasing the bounty on the head of Nicolas Maduro to $25 million for drug trafficking charges.

On January 14, *The New York Times* ran an editorial by US conservative Bret Stephens, which suggests that a priority of US President Donald Trump in his second term should be "deposing the regime of Nicolás Maduro in Venezuela, through coercive diplomacy if possible or force if necessary."

Stephens states that "punitive" economic sanctions "didn't work" (besides causing economic collapse and a wave of mass migration), the bounty put on Maduro's head likely won't work, and an internal coup is improbable due to the military's loyalty. Thus, he argues, the only option left to achieve the goal that is "overdue, morally right, and in our national security interest," i.e. overthrowing a democratically elected foreign government, is a powerful threat of US military intervention, and the real thing, "if we must."

The threats and attacks against Venezuela are made after the world has witnessed fifteen months of Israel's brutal genocide against the Palestinian people in Gaza. Billions of people across the globe have seen images of decapitated children, bombings of refugee camps, hospitals, and schools, and other atrocities, day after day for fifteen months. The Israeli military leaders and government officials responsible for this genocide, some of whom are wanted by the International Criminal Court, are welcomed into the halls of the US government and greeted by officials who give them standing ovations and promises of more military aid, in complete defiance of international law.

The glaring contradiction is dizzying, but of course US policy has never been dictated by who is doing things "right" or "wrong."

So, why for the last twenty-five years has the US government, Democrat or Republican, seemingly had an obsessive fixation on Venezuela, dedicating significant time and resources to undermine and attack the country in diverse ways: from the over a thousand sanctions, to the seizing of Venezuela's sovereign assets, to the direct political and financial support to the far-right opposition?

That is precisely what this short book seeks to answer. A short and simple answer is oil, but it is much more than that. The Bolivarian Revolution is not just a project that nationalized oil for the good of the nation, but it has embarked on a process to completely transform society, not only within Venezuela, but in the region and even across the world by giving a concrete basis for the ideals of solidarity, humanism, internationalism, and sovereignty.

The true answer to our question is one that can only be understood by considering multiple perspectives. In this volume we brought together pieces from analysts and political leaders from Venezuela and Latin America to explore different aspects of why the Bolivarian Revolution has caused the US empire to tremble.

In editing this volume, we encountered some difficulties—how does one translate the Bolivarian Revolution, with conceptual pillars that are so internal to Venezuela and its process, that any translation loses some of the historical references and essence?

We did our best to do justice to these concepts and framings and have also prepared a short glossary for reference.

The hope is that this volume will not only give you better grounds to understand the US offensive on Venezuela, but also, most importantly, why after twenty-five years of attacks, the Bolivarian Revolution is still standing strong and the Venezuelan people stand firm against imperialism.

GLOSSARY

4F: In the early hours of February 4, 1992, in an attempt to overthrow the anti-people and corrupt government of President Carlos Andrés Pérez, five army units led by young Lieutenant Colonel Hugo Chávez moved into Caracas to seize key military bases and communications installations throughout the city.

Supported by the civilian population, the rebel forces made swift advances and took control of large cities such as Valencia, Maracaibo, and Maracay. However, Chávez soon gave himself up to the government to avoid unnecessary deaths. After doing so, he was allowed to speak on national television, through which he addressed the fellow rebels and assured them that they had only failed "for now," subtly indicating towards the social revolution to come. The rebellion did not succeed, however, it kindled hope for change in Venezuelans and gave them a leader who could guide them in the process.

ALBA-TCP: Founded in 2004 with an agreement between presidents Hugo Chavez of Venezuela and Fidel Castro of Cuba, it is a regional platform that proposes a process of regional integration through strengthening political unity, promoting and working towards the program of Twenty-first Century Socialism, defending national sovereignty against US interventions, and working to address poverty, illiteracy, and the rights of indigenous and marginalized populations. ALBA is considered to be instrumental in blocking the realization of the FTAA and continues to drive efforts to lessen the grip of US imperialism in the region.

ALCA/FTAA: A trade agreement proposed in 1994 by US president Bill Clinton that would eliminate trade barriers between the US and all countries of the Americas, excluding Cuba. This would effectively create a US-led economic bloc against Cuba, prevent regional integration, and facilitate neoliberal imposition across the continent. It was strongly opposed by popular movements across the region, and Venezuelan president Hugo Chávez was one of its most vocal critics. Negotiations failed to reach an agreement and ended in failure in 2005.

Bolivarian Revolution: A political process inaugurated by Commander Hugo Chávez Frías in 1999 based on the premise that the resources of Venezuela could be used for the people of Venezuela to build another type of society where the basic aspects of human life are not commodified. This process vindicated its own anti-colonialist tradition by renewing the ideas of Simón Bolívar (1783–1830)—the struggle for independence, the struggle for the unity of the Latin American nation, and the struggle for social justice. On January 30, 2005, Chávez declared the socialist character of the Bolivarian Revolution and affirmed that it was necessary to transcend capitalism through socialism.

Caracazo: Known as one of the first uprisings against neoliberalism, on February 27, 1989, hundreds of thousands of poor Venezuelans took to the streets of Caracas following the increase in the price of basic food products, fuel, public transportation, and other public services. The increases were imposed after President Carlos Andrés Pérez signed a deal with the International Monetary Fund (IMF) in 1989.

In the face of insurrection, Pérez decreed a state of emergency and suspended all constitutional guarantees to citizens. The government deployed the military and permitted soldiers to use firearms against protesters, unleashing a brutal repression that resulted in the deaths of over three thousand people.

Civic-military union: A concept forged within the Bolivarian National Armed Forces (FANB) that seeks the integration and cooperation of the people and the military, to jointly defend the sovereignty and peace of Venezuela from the interventionist actions and aggressions of the US and its allies.

Communal Councils: Deliberative bodies where local community representatives propose, discuss and decide on public projects and initiatives and address issues the community is facing. Communal councils encompass from two hundred to four hundred families in urban areas or twenty to fifty families in rural areas. There are over forty-seven thousand registered communal councils in Venezuela. They are the cornerstones of building the communal socialism and communal state dreamed of by Chávez.

Hybrid war on Venezuela: The United States has used this new strategy to target governments that are hostile to US hegemony. This hybrid war—rather than a conventional war—allows the US to exploit the political, economic, and military weakness and limitations of the governments in the region. In Venezuela this has taken the shape of: economic and financial suffocation through sanctions/unilateral coercive measures, economic destabilization, media and diplomatic blockades, the promotion of violence inside the country—including assassinations—the generation of chaos with the attack on essential services (including the electricity grid), the pressure for an institutional fracture or a coup d'état and, finally, the threat of an external military intervention.

Nuestra América (Our America): Nuestra América, or "Our America," is a phrase that refers to a political project to unify the territory of Latin America first against European and then against US-led imperialism. The concept was first introduced by José Martí in 1891.

Participatory and protagonistic democracy: The model of democracy in the Bolivarian Revolution wherein people have direct partici-

pation and are leading agents of their own transformation, as opposed
to representative democracy. In this model, it is the people—latent,
living leaders—who are the true and original constituent power.
Within this framework, the institutional structures and the government must always be democratic, participatory, and decentralized.

Patria Grande (Great Homeland): Vision of the liberator Simón
Bolívar for a free, sovereign, and united Latin America that could face
the imperialist powers of the north with unity and strength.

Punto Fijo Pact (also referred to as Puntofijo Pact): A political alliance signed on October 31, 1958 between the Democratic Action
party, Copei (the Social Christian party), and Democratic Republican
Union party (URD), in order to guarantee political stability following a series of military coup governments and dictatorships. The pact
in name seeks to guarantee a transition to democratic life and rule of
law, but is between the status quo parties and excludes left sectors and
the Communist Party of Venezuela.

WHY VENEZUELA?

HOW THE US TRIES TO UNDERMINE DEMOCRACY AND SOVEREIGNTY IN LATIN AMERICA

THE BOLIVARIAN REVOLUTION: PAST, PRESENT, AND FUTURE

BY BLANCA EEKHOUT

Blanca Eekhout is a Deputy of the National Assembly of Venezuela and the President of the Simón Bolívar Institute.

The Bolivarian Revolution is the result of a historical process and a historical project. Bolívar's struggle is the synthesis of the Indigenous resistance. It is also the struggle of the Afro-descendant people who, in this land, become marooned people. It is the struggle for independence and the unity of all in the War of Independence, then in the Federal War, and the entire process of resistance and confrontation with the new, brutal, and savage model of colonization by North American imperialism against the entire region.

The Bolivarian Revolution is also the synthesis of the peoples' struggle for Latin American unity. So yes, it is an extraordinary and complex historical process.

Perhaps we can speak of a crucial moment. On February 27 and 28, 1989, the uprising of the people in the *Caracazo*. While the world proclaimed the end of history, it was the zenith of capitalism, the declaration of neoliberalism as the final stage of human development. They said it was the end of utopias. There was nothing more to fight for, and this terrible model of maximum exploitation of our peoples advanced brutally in the world.

In Venezuela, Carlos Andrés Pérez came to power within the framework of the Puntofijo Pact,[1] which had been in effect for forty years, and based on the pact made with the United States and with the parties Acción Democrática and Copei. At that time, after his victory, he declared that all the demands of the International Monetary Fund

---

1   A 1958 political alliance. see Glossary

and the World Bank would be fulfilled in Venezuela, and the package of economic measures from the IMF's deadly recipe would be applied.

At that moment, there was a response from the people, an overwhelming response, without organization, without clear objectives, but nevertheless a gigantic national mobilization that ended in looting and culminated in a criminal and genocidal act, with reported casualties of up to 3,600 deaths over those two days, February 27 and 28. There are figures that claim that 10,000 people were killed. Among them were men, women, children, many in their homes, as gunfire was directed at residential buildings using military-grade weapons. It was as if an occupying army had arrived in the country; it was a brutal, disproportionate action.

But it marks a milestone because, until that moment, Venezuela had been considered internationally—according to the media campaigns of the time—as an example of bourgeois democracy, of representative democracy. But it was an example of democracy where every five years the people were only partially invited, not all the people, limiting electoral participation greatly such that the exercise was often effectively prevented or the people's vote was defrauded. But above all, they were processes wherein all campaigns and commitments were absolutely unfulfilled, and sovereignty was limited to that one event where they could participate: the electoral event.

February 27 and 28 marked a milestone because they exposed that entire model and the criminal actions that persisted throughout the years of Puntofijo, the years of the Fourth Republic, and after the death of Father Bolívar. But particularly, it exposed that brutal period of the Puntofijo Pact, with its tutelage under the United States and the School of the Americas, with its brutal repression of the youth—the disappearance of much of that youth who rebelled against the handing over of the country—the handing over of its resources, the handing over of our territory.

And that was a global scandal. Perhaps it was one of the strongest uprisings against the recipe of the World Bank and the International Monetary Fund, and it was the most brutal repression that was committed, truly a genocidal criminal act against a defenseless people. National media outlets applauded the repression, fully siding with the genocidal government, which broke the spell, shattering the lie.

The media bubble was exposed as one of the fundamental elements supporting that criminal fascist regime. This immediately sparked an important reaction in popular organization, which later transformed into an unstoppable movement when Hugo Chávez appeared on the horizon.

THE EMERGENCE OF THE BOLIVARIAN MOVEMENT

In 1992, there was an uprising by the young military officers, a rebellion with limited civilian participation, mostly from university students and some leftist organizations, but primarily from the young officers of the National Armed Forces at that time. This rebellion, when it first appeared, did not have full popular support, as the people had been brutally repressed by those same forces. It was when Commander Hugo Chávez took the stage that the people were able to link these two actions: the 1989 uprising and the 1992 civic-military rebellion. When Chávez spoke, he introduced us to this Bolivarian movement and gave it all its historical depth.

At that time, there was also a cultural movement that began in the 1980s, and in 1983, it was the bicentennial of Father Bolívar's birth. This cultural movement of singers, called the Bolivarian Song, was led by Alí Primera, the people's singer, a man who unified the struggles of our people through his songs and actions. So, it was this cultural movement that was latent throughout the territory, which then experienced a moment of rupture with the false democracy in 1989.

At the moment Hugo Chávez appeared, he had a project, a possibility of a path forward, and it was at that moment, when he took the stage, to tell us about this Bolivarian movement. This movement is not an isolated act; it is a movement that proposed a way forward. At that moment, he had the capacity, even in a moment of surrender, when he was detained, to tell us that we had not yet achieved what he described, but that the country would head toward a different destiny and he assumed responsibility. This also carries significant weight because the political actions of that entire period—a brutal bureaucratic handover of the country to North American interests— were marked by a political practice where no one took responsibility for anything. Everything was deceit, lies, theft, and plundering of the people, their dreams, and their territory. So, indeed, this brave and courageous act, wherein he also assumes responsibility, made it clear that times would change, but that it came with Bolívar and was a movement.

This was decisive and unstoppable, and it marked the destiny of the Bolivarian Revolution. It was a long road from 1992, with imprisonment and persecution, until the great victory of 1998 and then the inauguration, which was also a significant political milestone. When Commander Chávez took office in February 1999, he did so with an oath, "I swear before this moribund Constitution," signaling the death of the old model and calling on the people. This is also important because, honoring his campaign, Bolívar was almost always present. Bolívar in his speech before the Congress of Venezuela in Angostura on February 15, 1819, proclaimed: "Happy is the citizen who, with the shield of arms under his command, calls upon the people to exercise their absolute will, their sovereignty."

And that is exactly what Commander Chávez did when he assumed the presidency of the National Government. When he swore before this moribund Constitution, he called us to draft the new legal framework of the Republic. He said, "We are going to re-found the Republic," and called for a constituent process, a consultation to hold a constituent assembly where, from that moment on, the peoples who for five hundred years had been long neglected—our Indigenous peoples, our Afro-descendant people, our workers, and peasants— who had reached an extraordinary pinnacle with the struggle and victory of the War of Independence but were immediately betrayed, would participate.

So, that centuries-long struggle reached a moment of fruition. It was precisely when Commander Chávez called on all the people of resistance, struggle, dreams, and life to build the legal framework of the Republic. It was an extraordinary process that we must always mention because, for the first time, a Constitution captured the dreams, aspirations, struggles, searches, and paths of our people.

And that Constitution, in Article Five, states: "Sovereignty resides intransferably in the people, who exercise it directly in the manner provided by this Constitution and the law, and indirectly through voting, by the bodies that exercise Public Power."

Thus, this marks our vision of the model of participatory and protagonistic democracy, of revolutionary democracy, of popular democracy. And this is the great battle we have fought over these years and continue to fight, not only for Venezuela. We believe it is indeed a necessity for humanity.

BUILDING THE REVOLUTION

The Bolivarian Revolution, as soon as Commander Chávez took office, faced a very complex situation. The country was in debt, mortgaged by the International Monetary Fund, and the price of oil was $7 a barrel. Venezuela, like all economies under that brutal form of neocolonialism dependent on North American imperialism, had become a monoproductive economy. This caused enormous damage when Commander Chávez arrived.

Poverty in Venezuela was a serious problem. Extreme poverty was at 40 percent. General poverty was over 60 percent. There was no way to pay the workers—the public administration employees—and there was enormous precariousness added to the historical debts of education, health, housing for our people, and the levels of marginality.

All services were being set up for privatization according to the neoliberal scheme: electricity, water, and services like education and health. So, the state was engaging in almost suicidal actions to carry out the entire privatization process.

And, as was said, the vast majority of the population living in neighborhoods, in popular communities, were condemned to be on the margins of these services, in communities that had never had access to drinking water or electricity. It was a truly complex and difficult situation. So, what was the role at that moment? Commander Chávez had called us, first of all, amidst so many needs, to rise up and reach a higher level of consciousness.

What we were experiencing was a product of a society built upon colonization and dependency, an exclusionary model and an undemocratic model. Bourgeois democracy is not democracy; it is a farce that kidnaps the sovereignty of the people. So, the first thing Commander Chávez proposed amidst such adversity was to refound the Republic. But with the law and the Constitution already in place, how do you address the historical debts?

One of the crucial elements in the exercise of government, amidst so many difficulties, was that each need had to be turned into an organization and each organization into a movement.

So what to do? Given the precariousness, what could be the immediate governmental action to put the state at the service of the people?

Commander Chávez created an initial mission, Plan Bolívar 2000,
and deployed all the National Armed Forces, the only organized structure in the territory, to attend to the people. The military was tasked
with implementing education programs, ensuring the distribution of
identity cards, providing dental evaluations, and delivering food to the
most remote communities. The goal was to demonstrate that the state
could serve the people, in contrast to the past when the Armed Forces
served the oligarchies to repress and murder the people.

This immediately changed the purpose of the state. It was now to
serve the people. But Commander Chávez also emphasized that it was
the people who needed to seize power, and for that reason, he said that
every need had to become an organization.

The people had no ownership of the land they inhabited, so they
could be dispossessed at any moment. They couldn't build homes or
farms because they owned nothing. Thus, one of the forms of organization in the territory was the Land Committees, starting with urban
lands where large, densely populated areas considered marginal—the
so-called misery belts—were actually where the majority of the city's
population lived.

In these areas, land committees were established so people could
rebuild their lives, asking themselves where they came from. Many
were from rural exoduses who had abandoned their land and ended
up in the only spaces that offered any possibility of life. Therefore, our
rural population ended up in these belts surrounding the large cities,
which once experienced the oil bonanza.

The organization of the Urban Land Committee (UTC) began to
reconstruct their origins, their identity, and, most importantly, the life
they wanted. Ownership was established by mapping out their neighborhoods, creating a historical record, and drafting a founding charter
for the neighborhood. The committee then became the organization
and, from there, a means to achieve goals.

Now, there was collective and family ownership, and the focus
shifted to what the Health Committees would do, since access to
health services was lacking. For the first time, doctors arrived in our
neighborhoods, fields, and Indigenous communities. During this

initial phase, Cuban doctors came with us, but the Health Committee was organized by the community.

Each committee—whether for health, education, housing, or water—transformed into an organization. The Water Technical Tables, Health Committees, and various forms of organization became crucial forces for transforming reality.

Commander Chávez told us that all these forms of organization needed the potential to become territorial governance. Thus, communal councils were created, grouping together the Land Committee, Water Committee, Health Committee, Education Committee, and Housing Committee into a powerful popular organization that then became a governing body—the communal council—and ultimately evolved into communes.

These communal councils often shared facilities like schools or health centers. Thus, there was a need to consolidate into a higher instance, in this case, the communes, where a fundamental element for the development of this power was linked to productive activity. We needed to organize to produce in the territory and to develop all its potential.

This is within the framework of those three roots: Bolívar's, which affirms that sovereignty resides in the people; Simón Rodríguez's, which tells us that the power of the people lies in their place. We either invent or err, because repeating old models imposed upon us is where the mistake lies. Only through heroic creation, through the invention of the people according to their needs, their searches, and their reality, will we find success.

Moreover, we must also look at that other deep root, the zamorano root, from Ezequiel Zamora, who, in the midst of the Federal War, told us, "We did not come to this war to choose who will rule the people, but for the people to rule, for the people to govern." Thus, the challenge was how to organize ourselves in the territory to build popular government, people's power, not just as a decree or a law in the Constitution, but as a permanent exercise of development. We began to walk on our own feet and build with our own hands, to think about ourselves according to our reality, not just from a place of need, but from a plan that would allow us to live a dignified life, our dream built collectively. This is crucial because it was done in parallel.

To boost and develop these people's struggles, it was necessary to generate income. In a country shattered by the neoliberal model, it was essential to recover oil prices. Through the Constituent Assembly, we managed to pass laws that ensured oil revenues would be directed to the nation, not to foreign interests. The enabling laws and hydrocarbon laws allowed us to regain control over the oil company and allocate its profits to the people. However, resources were needed for the Organization of the Petroleum Exporting Countries (OPEC) so that oil prices, which at the time were so low, could reach a fair level that ensured justice—a fair price that guaranteed the development of oil-producing countries, which were then being hit hard, especially countries like us, in that category of dependence and imperialist control as brutal as what was imposed on us.

So, while the internal forces of Popular Power were developing, organizing, mobilizing, and building a new model of democracy—participatory and protagonist—Commander Chávez was fighting to reunify OPEC. Commander Chávez achieved something that seemed unprecedented after the Gulf Wars, as he managed to bring together Iran, Iraq, and the rest of the oil-producing countries, including Kuwait. The Commander crossed deserts in an Iraq that was under siege, meeting with Saddam Hussein, and they reestablished that important mechanism within OPEC which allowed many countries around the world, including some not part of the organization, to recover the price of raw materials.

In Russia's case, for example, without the Bolivarian Revolution and Commander Chávez's titanic efforts to restore fair oil prices, Russia's own recovery would have been nearly impossible. Thus, what Venezuela did at that time was crucial. Meanwhile, it was already reestablishing connections for the greater goal of the Bolivarian Revolution, which is Latin American unity.

THE GREAT HOMELAND

There, the seeds were planted for what would later become Petrocaribe, ALBA (Bolivarian Alliance for the Peoples of Our America), CELAC (Community of Latin American and Caribbean States), and UNASUR (Union of South American Nations), as we found a way out of the pit and helped other nations, which is exactly what was done. As soon as Venezuela achieved stability, it managed to free Argentina from the horrific debt that condemned it to war, dependence, and barbarism. It was Venezuela that secured stability by purchasing Argentina's debt. In other words, as soon as our oil resources became sovereign and under our control, they were enhanced and used to develop national productive forces, while also providing immediate aid to the Caribbean, which was in a very difficult situation, and to the southern regions that needed support. At times, that same oil was sent to the United States, to the poor in the Bronx or to those who were devastated by Hurricane Katrina.

In this way, Venezuela developed its strength for solidarity and for the unity of the peoples. Venezuela opened spaces for dialogue with the entire world, always showing great respect for the unique realities of different countries. Particularly under Commander Chávez and later under President Maduro, Venezuela has always extended its arms for dialogue and engagement with the peoples of the world, including the United States, on a permanent basis. Perhaps one of the key points of President Nicolás Maduro's government has been the ongoing call for dialogue, dialogue above all else.

However, it is important to emphasize that the attacks on Venezuela have not been due to that diplomacy, which I mentioned, as it has been marked by dialogue. It is a Bolivarian diplomacy, one that understands the need for deep bonds among humanity and that the great threats facing humanity can only be overcome if we unite, together, as a people.

Within the framework of Bolivarian diplomacy, which is based on the solidarity of the peoples, it aims to change the paradigm of diplomacy, moving away from one based solely on the particular interests of a few groups, and instead embracing a diplomacy grounded in the belief that we inhabit a common Earth and that the destiny of each is the destiny of all. Only in that harmony, in that balance of the universe where peace prevails, can humanity, as Bolívar said, truly uncover the mysterious enigma of the human being in freedom. Achieving true freedom is the freedom of peace, of encounter, of equality, and of solidarity, where we are brothers and sisters, where we love one another, as Christ's commandment asks of us, to love one another.

For the Bolivarian Revolution, this is a quest, a task, and it is the fundamental reason why we march forward. First and foremost, we believe in Latin American unity and in the balance of the universe.

That's why we believe in a multipolar world, in a multicentric world. We understand the need to recognize each people, their history, their struggles, their vision for the future. And what will allow us to advance together is precisely breaking the mechanisms of domination, violence, and war, and avoiding the oppression of one people over another. The possibility of marching together in a world of equals is necessary, it is imperative, and it is the only way we have to preserve life on this planet.

A REVOLUTION UNDER SIEGE

We have enemies because, although Venezuela does not produce weapons of mass destruction and has never throughout its history invaded another country, when it did cross its borders two hundred years ago, it was to bring freedom without taking an inch of land from anyone. On the contrary, much of our land was, at some point, taken from us, as the British imperialists, in that horrendous alliance with the United States and ExxonMobil, now seek to do, using Guyana to claim the Essequibo. It is the oil companies that seek to seize this territory, intending to establish a military base and a focus of war in the region, not only for the exploitation of this vital territory, which is essential for life due to its delta, but also to exploit the oil of our Atlantic coast, the Venezuelan coast, and to occupy the entire region. Therefore, the defense of the Essequibo is crucial for regional peace, it is essential for life in the region, and it is fundamental to fully defending our sovereignty.

So yes, we have many enemies, but most importantly, as I mentioned, we do not possess weapons of mass destruction, but we have something that is very dangerous.

I suppose this is what inspired the infamous decree by Mr. Obama, which was later ratified by Mr. Trump and Mr. Biden, stating that Venezuela was an unusual and extraordinary threat. I believe they were referring to the model of true democracy, participatory and protagonist, the revolutionary democracy that allows the people to be protagonists and to govern.

We have terrible, brutal, and constant enemies who have kept us under siege, through criminal campaigns of demonization, persistent attempts at occupation, efforts to instigate civil war, and making life nearly impossible for our people. This has been systematic, permanent, since the attempted coup d'état. Before that, there were many actions aimed at sabotaging our economy during the first coup attempt, followed by the promotion of terrorist activities, occupations, the Operation Daktari in 2004, and the *guarimbas* (violent protests) involving Colombian paramilitary forces who were going to be disguised in the uniforms of the Bolivarian National Armed Forces to assassinate the president and create the conditions for a civil war.

This was the case throughout Commander President Hugo Chávez's administration, where he faced the most brutal international campaigns, including the disease that ultimately took his life—a plan by the enemies of this homeland who believed it would be the end of the Bolivarian Revolution. Commander Chávez not only defeated them despite his illness but also ensured unity by declaring from his heart, like a full moon: Nicolás Maduro. Nicolás, indeed a worker, but also a statesman, accompanied him in the construction of a multipolar and multicentric world, in the construction of Latin American unity and bridges to the rest of the world through ALBA, Petrocaribe, and UNASUR. This worker, trained in the labor movement and in the left, has had the courage, bravery, and wisdom to defend peace, the homeland, and to maintain the course of the Bolivarian Revolution during the most difficult times—times of renewed attempts at civil war, occupation, and mercenary invasions.

President Nicolás has managed to defend sovereignty in the face of those attempts through the creation of terrorist actions, known here as *guarimba*, which are criminal fascist actions. President Nicolás convened a Constituent process, just as Chávez did, following Bolívar's legacy of calling upon the people: "I trust the wisdom of the people more than the counsel of the wise," Bolívar said. We achieved peace and have resisted the entire multifactorial war strategy: economic war, cognitive war, and cultural war.

In that first phase of the economic war, intending for our country to fall into civil war due to famine, President Nicolás, following Commander Chávez's model, once again returned to the people. It is there, with the people, that the great solutions are found. He created the Local Supply and Production Committees (CLAP). When there was little to distribute, that distribution could not be done by the capitalist market, nor could the State do it above the people—it had

to be done by the people themselves. These committees were essential
in confronting the difficulties.

Similarly, during the pandemic that caused devastation worldwide,
with predictions from the United States and *The New York Times* that
we would become the epicenter of the pandemic, they had, with the
blockade, prevented medicines from reaching our country. They had
waged a systematic war to dismantle our health-care system, and with
the state weakened by the blockade, they created the conditions for
Venezuela to suffer brutally during the pandemic.

But they failed, and they failed because President Nicolás, with the
wisdom of the people and trust in the people, addressed the pandemic
not through conventional means but through popular organization,
optimizing resources and ensuring that in this country, where there
is a social mapping of the people, everyone knows the territory they
inhabit. But not only that, they know every inhabitant—each person
is not a statistic but a human being, knowing that there is a pregnant
woman, an elderly person, someone with a disability, someone with
four children, or a person with hypertension. This real knowledge,
because we are all protagonists of our lives, allowed us to develop a
health policy tailored to each territory. It made us one of the countries
with the lowest infection rates and mortality rates, in contrast, unfortunately, to the United States of America.

We managed to defeat the blockade with the diplomacy of the
people. Solidarity prevailed, which is our vision. Vaccines came to
us from Cuba, that Cuba which resists and works miracles. Vaccines
came from China, vaccines came from Russia. And despite being
robbed even of the money we paid to the World Health Organization
for vaccines, solidarity prevailed.

It is the people who can work the miracle of life, the miracle of
peace, and the miracle of true and real democracy, which should not
only exist within each country but across the entire world. Every
people has the right to decide their own destiny. Every people has the
right to live in peace, to restore bonds of solidarity rather than subju-
gation and domination.

So, why are there so many enemies against a people who have
only sought peace? Why this massive campaign? Why the blockade?
Because the more than nine hundred unilateral coercive measures,

which they call sanctions, are acts of war. Why are they waging this war against us?

I believe it is because of the example we set. If participatory and protagonist democracy, direct democracy, triumphs—if it brings happiness, life, and development—then it becomes a bad example, because the criminal plutocracy that governs the United States feels threatened.

If the North American people were to truly realize the possibility of building a true democracy, one that is not determined by lobbyists, not controlled by the super wealthy, but by the right of every person to exercise power in the territory of the people's power, in the place where they decide to live with dignity and regain the right to be the protagonist of their own history and destiny—then that is what I believe Obama, Trump, and Biden considered in their infamous decrees. "An unusual and extraordinary threat." But we are convinced that this is the only path to sustaining life on this planet. The right of the people to decide, for dialogue and coexistence to prevail, and for this model of true democracy to triumph—the people's democracy, not the elites' democracy. Direct democracy, not representative democracy. A democracy that is exercised daily, not postponed every five years. That is what makes us an unusual and extraordinary threat.

We must build a different world where solidarity prevails. To live in communion, in community. And that requires weaving bonds of brotherhood. It is love that must prevail, and the force that will allow us to save life on this planet is love, and we must fight for it. Love is woven in peace, not in war. We must preserve peace and build these bonds, these ties of love between peoples—the destiny of one is the destiny of all. Humanity will not survive unless it lives on a living planet where life has value. And this is an essential task. We must defend the practice of true democracy—direct, revolutionary democracy. We must defeat deceit and lies, and we must restore communication between human beings, beyond the dictatorship of the media or the dictatorship of social networks, which only lead us to hatred, war, and destruction.

CHAVISMO AS A GRASSROOTS MOVEMENT: POPULAR POWER AS THE ENGINE OF THE BOLIVARIAN REVOLUTION

BY HERNÁN JOSÉ VARGAS PÉREZ

Hernán José Vargas Pérez is a militant of the organization Residential Workers United for Venezuela, a spokesperson for the Movement of Urban Struggles, an investigator and cofounder of the Venezuelan Observatory of Popular Economies, a member of the political coordination of ALBA Movimientos, and the former vice minister of Communal Economy.

Venezuela began a path of transformations with a constituent process in 1999 that marked a new era of refoundation of the Republic. This included a new paradigm of "participatory and protagonist democracy,"[1] an oil reform that recovered national income and used it for social investment, and an economy with state regulation of the free market and emphasis on labor and consumption of the great majorities. Looking outwards, there was a fierce questioning of imperialism and its neoliberal integration project, meanwhile Venezuela promoted integration within Latin America and the Caribbean and with the countries of the world that are not aligned with Global North interests, demanding respect for sovereignty and cooperation for a new development framework.

The Bolivarian Republic of Venezuela emerged as a political project centered on the doctrine of Simón Bolívar *the Liberator*, Simón Rodríguez *the Teacher*, and Ezequiel Zamora *the People's General*. Its first ideological coordinates relate to independence heroes. In time it was defined as a socialist project. Commander Hugo Chávez proposed the thesis of a territorial socialism centered on the commune, in the construction of Popular Power, which has undeniably impacted the political practice of both state and government institutions, political parties, as well as popular movements and grassroots organizations. As a result, Chavismo has configured itself not only as a movement of

---

1   A new democratic paradigm, moving from a representative system towards one of self-governance.

Chávez supporters but as the common ground of a set of grassroots movements. For example: (i) the Socialist Party of Venezuela has a structure that reaches every street in the country; (ii) in almost every community there is a Communal Council or a Commune; (iii) as well as very influential social movements, trade unions, and religious and cultural networks that supports Bolivarian Revolution.

POLITICAL DEFINITIONS: WHAT IS THIS SOCIALISM FROM THE COMMUNE?

The proposal made by Hugo Chávez and later continued by Nicolás Maduro is one of unprecedented complexity, because it places the *people* in a central place, beyond just being the object of policy that will benefit them. It also goes beyond the politicians who promise they will change things for you. It literally states that it must be the Popular Power that destroys the structures and webs of capitalism and its form of state while building the alternative forms of socialism to manage politics, planning, and production of life:

> To advance towards socialism we need a popular power capable of dismantling the plots of oppression, exploitation, and domination that subsist in Venezuelan society, capable of configuring new social relations from everyday life where fraternity and solidarity run together with the permanent emergence of new ways of planning and producing the material life of our people. This involves completely pulverizing the form of the bourgeois state we inherited, which still reproduces itself through its old and harmful practices, and giving continuity to the invention of new forms of political management.
>
> — *Hugo Chávez, Presentation of the Government Program for the period 2012–2018.*

Under this premise, Commander Chávez questioned his government cabinet in a famous public speech known as *Golpe de Timón* (Strike at the Helm) in 2012, where he basically proposed a turnaround to management in order to guarantee that everything done by the revolution contribute to the construction of the commune as the fundamental cell of socialism. In that sense, he tries to establish a reference to evaluate if we are advancing in the construction of socialism or not:

> The standard of measurement—says Mészáros—of socialist achievements is: to what degree the measures and policies adopted actively contribute to the constitution and well-rooted consolidation of a substantially democratic mode of social control and general self-management.
>
> — *Hugo Chávez, Golpe de Timón,*
> *Council of Ministers of the new cycle of the Bolivarian*
> *Revolution, 2012*

This idea complements well with the previous one: if we read in the context of the complete speech and also complement it with the work of Mészáros, we find seminal ideas of a doctrine that states that in territorial socialism, the people organized in popular power must have social control of the means of production and economic planning to guarantee that this responds to the material needs of life of the people who produce. This guideline consequently implies the constitution of a productive model centered on generalized self-management in all the links of the value chain, meaning that the people not only decide what is produced and for whom, but also they produce it directly. In this conception, substantive democracy merges politics and economics, the material conditions for a model of society where the people have no intermediaries to exercise their sovereignty. Chávez quoted Bolívar when he said "Independence or Nothing," and immediately completed *"Comuna o nada"* ("Commune or Nothing") as a premise that complements and updates the Bolivarian project: without the commune there is no independence.

STRATEGY AND PROGRAM: RIGHTS-POLICIES-POPULAR ORGANIZATION

There are probably two concrete expressions that have distinguished Chavismo from other political movements that have even promoted constituent processes in the region: on the one hand, the promotion of the organization of a popular subject as a component of each sectoral or general policy promoted by the state; and on the other hand, making this organized subject a direct executor of public resources. Let us look at some strategic policies that serve as examples of how these dynamics have operated.

In 2000, the Constitution of the Bolivarian Republic of Venezuela was approved. It recognizes the right of the people to access water, and with its approval, began a process to cease the privatization of services that was underway. In contrast, a process of both recovery and expansion of water supply system infrastructure networks was undertaken, and within the water service companies there was a shift away from traditional managerial guidelines, instead towards community control. Under Chavista administration, they called for the creation of technical boards on water where the community itself defined people who would be in charge of carrying out diagnoses of water networks and mapping of the conditions of access in all sectors of the community. Then from there, they would develop community projects for the connection, maintenance, and expansion of existing water networks, as well as the progressive development of new networks with aqueduct systems, deep wells, community tanks, among others. As time went by, the water companies became structures for training, technical advice, and logistical support for the formulation and execution of community water projects.

In 2003, after noting the enormous need for medical attention for the Venezuelan people, the Bolivarian government decided to develop, within the framework of the cooperation agreement with the Republic of Cuba, a state policy to guarantee health care to the most vulnerable sectors of the population. The *Barrio Adentro Mission* was created to guarantee preventive medicine, primary care, and of course, permanent specialized care for acute, sub-acute, and chronic diseases. The organization of *health community committees* in all Venezuelan neighborhoods and towns was fundamental for the mission's fulfillment, with the objective of cooperating with the medical personnel assigned to each neighborhood to survey needs, take a census of illnesses, organize special days for health care, and regular consultation schedules. This practice created the possibility for development of the *health community committees* that could plan and execute plans for disease prevention and pest and epidemic control, as well as to promote the community's involvement in the construction, adaptation, and provision of health centers with the support of the state.

In 2004, a law was enacted for the regularization of land in urban popular settlements, these being the areas where more than 80 percent of the Venezuelan population is located; this law seeks to implement the right of access to land, housing and a decent habitat guaranteed by the national constitution. The national policy for urban land had as its central point of departure, the organization of urban land committees (CTU) in each neighborhood of the country. The community elected its members who would have the task of systematizing the history of the neighborhood, the chain of land ownership titles, and the register of the territory; all this generates the legal requirements for each family of the community to legalize the tenure of the land they have inhabited for years, in this way more than one million families have been regularized under the joint effort of the CTU and the Venezuelan State.

Similar experiences occurred in relation to the right to education, the right to electric energy as well as telecommunications and technologies, and the rights of women to a life free of violence, among other areas of revolutionary policy that laid certain foundations to this thesis of a national project built by the popular power from the organized communities. During this time, the communities also developed methods, dynamics, technologies, and forms of management and governance that are co-responsible and co-managed, and have directly executed community projects financed with public resources, since part of the country's oil income goes to the Popular Power.

ORGANIC SYNTHESIS: COMMUNAL COUNCIL, COMMUNE, AND SOCIALISM

In 2005, a process of articulation of the three levels of the executive power began. These levels were the national government, regional governments, and municipal governments through a mechanism known as regional mobile cabinets. The purpose of these spaces was joint planning, identifying priority projects to be executed at each level but in a coordinated manner. This unprecedented experience in the country at that time was a test in the search for political efficiency and revolutionary quality mentioned by Alfredo Maneiro. Progress was made in the necessary coordination but there were two important conclusions: One explicit, one where Commander Chávez questioned the pertinence of the projects prioritized among ministers, governors and mayors, due to the impact they generated in the territories and the validation of the people; another conclusion which was not explicit was that months later, Commander Chávez decided to create the Communal Councils as instances where each community elected spokespersons who could formulate priority community projects for territorial development.

In 2006, the Communal Councils (CC) were created as instances of participation so that the organized people could directly exercise the management of public policies and community development projects. The organic definition assumed that the diversity of committees and technical boards of the community should integrate the CC. One of the most interesting definitions of this structure is that the spokespersons are elected by direct and secret vote in general elections where the whole community participates; however, what they elect are spokespersons that serve the collective mandate; they are not representatives. According to the law, the highest instance of a CC is the citizens' assembly, to which its spokespersons are obliged to submit to its decisions in the exercise of a communal cycle where the community diagnoses, plans, formulates projects, executes, and evaluates.

After three years of CC organization and state financing for the execution of community projects for the recovery, expansion, and creation of infrastructure networks in education, health, roads, water, electricity, sports, culture, economy, among many others, Commander Chávez oriented the creation of Communes as founding cells of socialism where several CC are added so that popular power may exercise self-government to configure a new society in five fronts:

> Moral: the conscience of social duty to combat selfishness and individualism instilled by capitalism.

> Social: to each according to his needs, from each according to his abilities; equality as the basis of socialist and territorial society.

> Political: greater levels of popular power, of self-government, to legislate and govern democratically.

Economic: a commune without a factory, without land, without socialist commerce is not a commune; the means of production must be in the hands of the commune.

Territorial: to build socialism from below, taking possession of the space and demanding the transfer of power.

— *Hugo Chávez, Aló Teórico #1, 2009*

CHALLENGES OF CHAVISMO IN A NEW PERIOD

1. Recognize Chavismo as a Historic Movement that Proposes a New Model of Society

Professor Iraida Vargas and Professor Mario Sanoja have worked much of their lives on a fundamental thesis: Bolivarian socialism is and will be the result of a long march towards communal society. This march begins with the Indigenous communities whose communal civilizational model was not erased by the European genocide on our lands. The communal form was the basis of defense in Indigenous settlements and Afro *Cumbes*, which over time became independence struggles, then peasant struggles, then guerrilla, student, workers, and neighborhood struggles. According to this thesis, the multiplicity of grassroots organizational forms that we have gone through since 1999 have been viable because we are the result of a historical accumulation of communal roots. Recognizing this thesis is a potentially decolonizing decision that could help us to break with our dependence on Eurocentric theories. These theories always lead us to try to reproduce a model of civilization that is in crisis, putting life at risk with its dynamics of imperial domination, natural depredation, repression and war, inequality, discrimination, and concentration of capital based on the dispossession of the majority. We cannot continue with this model. It is not necessary to change it but to demolish it, and our peoples have the capacity and foundations for the construction of a communal alternative.

2. Recognize Ourselves as a National Resistance Movement

If we affirm that our common root in Chavismo is the communal civilization, the next challenge is to recognize that our forms of organization have been multiple, different, diverse, and contradictory, but very possibly complementary.

Over the past decade, Venezuela has been subjected to more than nine hundred imperialist sanctions that have put society in shock. In response, we have developed organizational forms to resist. For example, in light of the goods and public budget shortages, the state structured a policy of direct distribution of subsidized food to most working families. For this, one of the fundamental principles of Chavismo was activated again, generating popular organization as a fundamental means to fulfill a mission. As a result, we have thousands of local supply and production committees (CLAP) that guarantee that basic food baskets reach six million families.

Hand in hand with this process, a party structure was strengthened which today reaches every street in Venezuela. It is a platform of territorial mobilization which among other things has allowed us to organize electoral participation in a very comprehensive way.

These organized grassroots forms have different but not antagonistic *modus operandi*. The unification of these forces allowed us to win the recent presidential elections. Understanding this complementarity is fundamental in order to work on the internal contradictions but always from a perspective of unity.

3. Recognizing Ourselves as a Communal Socialist Movement

If we make a summary of our journey, we could say that when it was our turn to guarantee rights through revolutionary policies, popular organization was decisive to achieve land regularization, access to education and health, water services, electricity, telecommunications, and productive financing. Then we could say that organizing the Communal Councils to exercise policies and projects in a self-managed way allowed us to find a way of redistributing national income within greater political efficiency and revolutionary quality. After a strong period of resistance to the blockade, we have expanded the organizational forms to guarantee food, territorial defense, and electoral mobilization, as well as multiple forms of organization for sectoral struggles of a great diversity of social movements.

A new period begins with a great accumulation of grassroots forces in a context of imperialist blockade, with fascist threats in the region, and an enormous need for changes and transformations.

Fifty-one percent of the Venezuelan people recently elected Nicolás Maduro to execute these changes. What is an effective and revolutionary strategy? Everything indicates that we must return to the moment of the *Golpe de Timón*, ratify that without commune there is no independence, and that the communal horizon does not only concern the CC and communes, but also the CLAP, the popular militia, the grassroots of the party, and the diversity of social movements that have granted us resistance.

All these unified forces have the task of assuming the next step in the long march of creating our communal society: our socialism requires confronting imperialism, fascism, and internal contradictions, all at the same time, within radical democracy, social control, and general self-management of the means necessary to produce the material life of our people.

THE HOMELAND IS AMERICA

VENEZUELA AND ITS COMMITMENT TO THE BOLIVARIAN DREAM OF CONTINENTAL UNITY AND INTEGRATION

BY LAURA CAPOTE

Laura Capote is a member of the Continental Operational Secretariat
of ALBA Movimientos and a militant of the Political and Social
Coordination Marcha Patriotica of Colombia.

"It has been almost two hundred years since Simón Bolívar's warning, and here we are, to continue saying: "No to
North American interventionism in our land."

— *Hugo Chávez, February 29, 2004.*

Venezuela's protagonism in designing a continental project of unity
and integration predates the Bolivarian Revolution by more than
two centuries. But in the Bolivarian Revolution, it finds its definitive
and renewed impetus in the struggle against US imperialism and its
hunger for control over Latin America and the Caribbean.

In 1815, the Liberator Simón Bolívar wrote the Letter of Jamaica,
articulating the Latin American doctrine of unity and sovereignty
that founded our first independence. In its pages, he developed the
key elements of what he considered fundamental for that project, a
common thread that remains as relevant as it was in the early nine-
teenth century: the need to achieve both political and economic
sovereignty of our countries, respect for the rights of all those who
inhabited our continent, and the recognition of the diversity of our
region as a potential unifying and revolutionary force.

But the Bolivarian ideology was betrayed by the local oligarchies. They set out to undermine unity which, more than a romantic
slogan, was a political strategy to free us from colonialism. Bolívar's
revolutionary project was left unfinished in the face of the nascent
imperialism of the United States which, in his words, had "plagued

America with misery in the name of freedom." However, more than two hundred years later—as Chilean poet-diplomat Pablo Neruda said—Bolívar was born again with the awakening of his people, in the same Venezuela, this time commanded by a *llanero* from Barinas who, trained in the Bolivarian doctrine together with the ideas of revolutionaries Ezequiel Zamora and Simón Rodríguez, promoted a new continental epic of integration.

Once again, a project arrived in our continent that, in addition to its ideas, took the name of the Liberator: this Bolivarian Revolution promoted—in a context of unrest for our peoples—the renewal of the project designed in the Letter of Jamaica and gave it a potential that is still in force today.

THE CONTEXT OF REINVIGORATION

Latin America and the Caribbean have historically played a leading role in shaping US interventionist policy on a global scale. Since the inception of the Monroe Doctrine, Washington declared the continent as part of its zone of influence in the Western Hemisphere, a position it maintained throughout the twentieth century. This position, consolidated first with the projects linked to the National Security Doctrine in the 1970s which sought to crush left forces, and then through the establishment of a neoliberal model in the 1990s, was challenged. The mass mobilizations, as well as social and political conquests of left and progressive forces on the continent during the first decade of this century, changed the course of events.

The arrival of the neoliberal model in Latin America and the Caribbean brought with it an economic and social crisis that deepened the levels of inequality in the region, cementing a model that benefited minorities at the expense of the popular classes. With this crisis on the rise, the beginning of the 1990s was a milestone, marking the beginning of what would be an eruption of popular anti-neoliberal mobilizations, which would divide the history of the struggle in the continent and bring the role of social and popular organizations to the forefront.

The UN Economic Commission for Latin America and the Caribbean (ECLAC) prepared an Economic Study of Latin America and the Caribbean in 1999. The report spoke to the role of the region in the concentration of US capital: "between 1990 and 1997, 48 percent of the 250 foreign firms in Latin America and the Caribbean were from the United States, and only 38.4 percent were European."[1] In turn, to comply with loan payments that resulted from economic agreements with multilateral organizations such as the International Monetary Fund (IMF) and the World Bank, Latin American governments applied measures to the detriment of the popular classes: by the end of 1990, the number of people living in poverty in Latin America and the Caribbean was 223 million people, almost 11 million more than in 1990. Additionally, in our region by the end of the decade, "42 million people were illiterate, 31 percent of children and young people did not attend school, 118 million children worked and between 40 and 50 million of that segment would be absorbed by delinquency, and 267 million Latin Americans and Caribbeans had no health services, in addition to 152 million without access to drinking water or sewage."

In this context, in February 1989, the *Caracazo* took place in Venezuela as a social outburst against the neoliberal measures of the government of Carlos Andrés Pérez. This insurrection inaugurated a period of struggles across the entire continent that bubbled up against the neoliberal model, joining the process initiated years earlier by different expressions of organization in defense of agrarian reform, such as the Landless Rural Workers Movement (MST) in Brazil, the Zapatista uprising in Mexico, the Water and Gas Wars in Bolivia, and the 2001 uprising in Argentina. While the United States saw itself as the victor after the collapse of the socialist bloc and the end of the Cold War, these uprisings renewed the stakes of the game.

The rise of Hugo Chávez to power in Venezuela marked a profound contrast to the regional structure of alliance or cooperation with the United States. In 1992, with the precedent of the *Caracazo*, Hugo Chávez led an initial coup attempt in Venezuela together with the Bolivarian Revolutionary Movement 200 which, in spite of its failure, opened the doors to a new political moment in the country.

---

1   ECLAC, Economic Survey of Latin America and the Caribbean 1998–1999. Retrieved from https://www.cepal.org/es/publicaciones/1044-estudio-economico-america-latina-ca-ribe-1998-1999

THE CENTRAL ROLE OF THE INTERNATIONAL AGENDA
IN HUGO CHÁVEZ'S PROJECT

After his unsuccessful coup attempt, Chávez dedicated himself to consolidating the V Republic Movement, a national project based on sovereignty and the return to Bolivarian principles. These principles founded, after Chávez's electoral triumph in 1998, a Venezuelan foreign policy oriented toward solidifying the independence movements in the region as a condition for the viability of the national project. This vision was embodied in the preamble of the Constitution of the Bolivarian Republic of Venezuela, promulgated a year later.[2] Likewise, this approach was developed in the document "Bolivarian Revolution. The New Stage. The New Strategic Map" of 2004, where the strategic objectives of the government of Hugo Chávez Frías are compiled:

> "To continue promoting the new multipolar and international system" is the framework within which the continental project is developed. [In Latin America] two opposing axes have been defined, Caracas, Brasilia, Buenos Aires . . . the axis we could call Orinoco–Amazonas–Río de la Plata. There is another axis. Bogotá–Quito–Lima–Santiago de Chile; this axis is dominated by the Pentagon . . . It is the Bolívar axis or the Monroe axis. Of course, our strategy must be to break that axis and build South American unity, and I believe that it is not a dream, I believe that never before in America has there been a situation like this.[3]

The three fundamental elements of the Bolivarian political project of regional scope could be summarized as follows: the retaking of the Bolivarian proposal as a central element of its national and foreign policy, the construction of a society where social and communal organization would guarantee the establishment of this project of

---

2   Constitution of the Bolivarian Republic of Venezuela. Retrieved from http://www.cne. gob.ve/web/normativa_electoral/constitucion/indice.php

3   Harnecker, Marta. *High level workshop "The new strategic map." Interventions by Hugo Chávez Frías.* 2004. Retrieved from https://www.urru.org/papers/El_nuevo_mapa_ estrategico.pdf

sovereignty, and the construction of the socialism of the twenty-first century for Venezuela and Latin America and the Caribbean.[4]

THE DEFEAT OF THE FTAA AS A PARADIGM

The development of an alternative project became one of the priorities of Bolivarian foreign policy. This is evident in Commander Hugo Chávez's opposition to the proposal of the Free Trade Area of the Americas (FTAA).

The United States had been promoting the FTAA in the region, seeking to establish the policy at the third Summit of the Americas in April 2001. The FTAA was an economic and trade treaty that sought to reduce tariff barriers and allow the US even greater access to markets, encouraging the privatization of public goods and services, greater foreign investment, among other measures that had already been imposed in the previous decade but in a fragmented way, on some countries of Latin America. Warning of the dangers that the plan posed for regional sovereignty, Venezuela, together with Cuba, led the call for a proposal for social, economic, political, and cultural integration of the peoples of Latin America and the Caribbean—a counterweight to the FTAA project.

Likewise, for the Chávez government it was fundamental to defeat the FTAA project again at the Summit of the Americas in Mar del Plata in 2005. Thus, a group of countries led by Venezuela and Argentina opposed the approval of the treaty, pointing to the inequalities between the economies of the region found with respect to the US economy, and the effects that this treaty would bring to the masses in the continent.

The defeat of the FTAA was a foundational event in a path of continental integration and articulation, a path that was just beginning. From then on, the group of countries that had managed to stop the treaty had a course to follow, creating a series of organizations that would bring together the political dynamics of the region.

Thus, with an alternative project to the neoliberal model, a progressive bloc emerged that promoted plans for regional integration. This not only strengthened the continent in political terms, but also improved it in a wide range of economic, commercial, and productive

---

4   Domínguez Guadarrama, Ricardo. Chávez and Latin American integration. Retrieved from https://core.ac.uk/download/pdf/322549392.pd

dimensions. It even created its own mechanisms that excluded the United States as a convenor or participant, unlike the Organization of American States (OAS).

These alternative projects to the neoliberal model were driven by popular anti-neoliberal insurrections, achieving political and electoral victories for ten continuous years, constituting "the won decade" in Latin America and the Caribbean.[5] In addition to the development of governments with progressive or revolutionary agendas, the era was also characterized by a continental understanding of the political moment and a special concern for promoting and strengthening regional integration mechanisms that would make it possible to build a project that encompassed the entire region and turned the page on neoliberalism.

Despite the differences among them, the progressive governments of Latin America and the Caribbean developed a series of measures focused on the fight against the enormous inequality and unemployment gap that the 1990s had created. Bolivia, Brazil, and Venezuela reduced poverty levels by more than half and advanced various processes of nationalization of natural resources and strategic sectors of the economy, all accompanied by sustained economic growth. In particular, the Venezuelan and Bolivian projects developed structural transformations through projects of socialism of the twenty-first century, focused on sovereignty and integration, consolidated through a process of constituent change. This allowed for the refounding of the national projects centered on the "V Republic" and the "Plurinational State" respectively.

In the global context, it was not insignificant that the Latin American and Caribbean processes retook slogans that seemed to have been buried by the end of the Cold War, as was the case with socialism and the anti-imperialist agenda. Within this framework, and together with Fidel Castro at the head of the Cuban Revolution, these revolutionary processes developed an alternative project to the one offered by Washington.

ALBA OFFERS A NEW HORIZON

The Bolivarian Republic of Venezuela was then in charge of building a Bolivarian Alternative Agenda for the entire region centered around

---

5   CELAG, *América latina, de la década ganada a la década disputada*, 2014. Retrieved from http://www.celag.org/wp-content/uploads/2014/03/Presentación-CELAG.pdf

sovereignty, integration, and social justice. This would later be concretized in the convergence of Bolivarian thinking and the proposal of the Socialism of the Twenty-First Century.

Venezuela spearheaded a regional project seeking not only to strengthen and consolidate existing regional mechanisms, but also to create new opportunities to remedy the pending promises for integration. Thus, in the context of the struggle against the FTAA, but also aiming to give substance to the Bolivarian proposal of the Revolution, Commander Hugo Chávez together with Fidel Castro inaugurated the Bolivarian Alternative for the Peoples of Our America—ALBA on December 14, 2004. ALBA would be the alternative project that would allow building a strategic political articulation with the objective of unity of the Great Homeland following the Bolivarian ideology and the *"principles of solidarity, cooperation, and complementarity among our countries."*[6]

Thus, ALBA emerged as a horizon for the cooperation of governments and peoples from a perspective of unity and internationalism among the peoples of the region. In the same sense, social and popular movements called upon other mass movements of the continent to also build a regional expression from the organized sectors of the Latin American and Caribbean peoples in the Charter of the Social Movements of Belém do Pará. This was not only to defend these principles of ALBA, but also to deepen them in the most revolutionary and transforming sense. This was expressed in the foundation of ALBA Movimientos, which to date has had the revolutionary governments of Cuba and Venezuela as its main allies.

Simultaneously, the Venezuelan government strengthened its continental strategy through the creation of multilateral organizations with a sovereign perspective. As is the case of the Union of South American Nations (UNASUR), founded in 2008, which sought to move away from the model championed by the OAS as the banner of Pan-Americanism, and instead expressing alternative agendas for politics and defense. Another example is the creation of the Community of Latin American and Caribbean States (CELAC) in 2011, which sought to articulate a regional agenda for the defense of Latin

---

6   León, Irene. *ALBA: Latin American horizon of the XXI Century*. 2013. Retrieved from https://www.alainet.org/sites/default/files/Libro_Alba.pdf

America and the Caribbean as a zone of peace,[7] and which today is strengthened thanks to the return of several key countries to the Community.

In the following years, Venezuela's momentum helped create a series of initiatives aimed at advancing the region toward a project of political and economic sovereignty, positioning it as a significant pole in the reconfiguration of global power and the emergence of a multipolar world. These include *TeleSUR*, a news agency fighting within the communication battle; the Bank of the South; and Petrocaribe, an alliance focused on providing Venezuelan oil to Caribbean countries under preferential payment conditions, in addition to fortifying the aforementioned regional institutions. This strengthening of the region also allowed it to enter into dialogue with the new actors emerging on the multipolar, multilateral scene, particularly with regard to the creation and promotion of the BRICS with the leading participation of Brazil.

Regarding ALBA-TCP, it is worth highlighting achievements that were fundamental for the countries now involved in the alliance, these include: the more than five million ophthalmological surgical interventions through the Miracle Operation (Operación Milagro), which restored sight to the beneficiaries; the implementation of a program providing more than one million technical aids for people with disabilities; the development of common literacy programs, which successfully taught approximately five million people; the professional training of more than twenty thousand community-integrated doctors at the Latin American School of Medicine, both in Cuba and Venezuela, among other measures.

And those of the aforementioned Platform of Social Movements towards ALBA (ALBA Movimientos), include the promotion of International Solidarity Brigades in Cuba, Venezuela, and Haiti and the building of the Continental System of Political Education among more than twenty schools and training and research processes of the movements in the continent. Also of note are the solidarity campaigns, such as *Pueblos Soberanos, Pueblos Solidarios* (Sovereign People, People Of Solidarity) against unilateral coercive measures,

7   Observatorio de Coyuntura de América Latina y el Caribe. Tricontinental Institute for Social Research. *Colombia, Venezuela and our second imperial frontier.* 2021. Retrieved from https://thetricontinental.org/argentina/obsalcuaderno4/

and In Defense of a Dignified, Sovereign Haiti Free of Occupation; *Cuba Vive y Resiste* (Let Cuba Live!) for the exclusion of Cuba from the list of countries sponsoring terrorism; as well as the campaign: For Democracy and Sovereignty: Hands Off Venezuela!

After the death of Hugo Chávez in Venezuela, this decade of blossoming social movements and electoral triumphs of progressive projects was met with a return of neoliberal-conservative projects in the governments of the region—precisely in those countries that had been key pieces in establishing continental expression. The struggle in Venezuela is not an electoral debate on democratic see-sawing alternation—it is a debate on models for the region. This struggle is fundamental to defending our continental sovereignty, in the context of our common goods being auctioned off, as in Argentina governed by Milei, or the permanent tours of the Head of the Southern Command in our countries.

That is why the defense of the Bolivarian Revolution is the task of continuing the unfinished and just project for our continent, left to us by the Liberator more than two hundred years ago. The great Bolivarian purpose was to transcend the mere anti-colonialist struggle for independence, and instead to also create from these new conditions a revolutionary, democratic, and transformative process of continental unity with the popular masses as the only protagonists. That is why, while they attempt to divide us, the people of Our America and the Bolivarian people respond with unity. The Liberator had already warned us in the Manifesto of Cartagena: "Our division, not Spanish weapons, have returned us to slavery." We do not have time, nor possibilities of making a mistake again.

UNITED STATES VS. BOLIVARIAN REVOLUTION

BY CARLOS RON

Carlos Ron is the former Venezuelan Vice Minister of Foreign Affairs for North America.

In 1829, a year before his death, Simón Bolívar, the leader of the South American independence movement and the inspiration for today's Bolivarian Revolution in Venezuela, wrote a prophetic phrase: *"The United States seems destined by Providence to plague America with misery in the name of Liberty."* Bolívar had dealt with a treacherous government in Washington which, despite stating their neutrality, had taken actions that favored the Spaniards. This is not surprising, considering it was always in the interest of the US that the independence movement didn't succeed. As early as 1786, Thomas Jefferson had written:

> Our confederacy must be viewed as the nest from which all America, North and South, is to be peopled. We should take care, too, not to think it for the interest of that great continent to press too soon on the Spaniards. Those countries cannot be in better hands. My fear is that they are too feeble to hold them till our population can be sufficiently advanced to gain it from them piece by piece.

This means that since the time of the founding of the two countries, the United States and Venezuela have had a tense relationship marked by two different projects for the same territory. The US project, as a neocolonial project based on the tradition of the Manifest Destiny, trying to expand its influence over South America; versus the Bolivarian project, as a project of political and social emancipation for its people. This tension has reached different highs and lows in a complex history of two hundred years, but it has never quite subsided.

The United States became a superpower after World War II, in part, with the help of Venezuelan oil. It helped install a fascist, anti-communist dictatorship in the 1950s until the victory of the Cuban Revolution pushed the US government to shift from its strategies of supporting brutal dictatorships to ones of establishing controlled democratic projects that would continue to ban the left's participation in politics. Venezuela became a role model for US allies—it was one of the countries visited by US President John F. Kennedy during his Alliance for Progress plan. As neoliberalism spread throughout Latin America, however, Venezuela reacted forcefully: first in 1989, with the popular uprising known as the *Caracazo* where the masses took the streets against the International Monetary Fund's (IMF) structural adjustment program, and later in 1992, with two military rebellions led by Hugo Chávez which showed that the liberal democracy model for Latin America had been shattered. By 1998, popular rejection of neoliberalism and the idea that democracy could be exercised by people and not just by elites, led to the election of Hugo Chávez as president and the writing of a new constitution that transformed the country into a participatory democracy.

CHÁVEZ CHARTS A NEW PATH OF SOVEREIGNTY

The United States initially reacted by underestimating Chávez and what he represented. The Clinton Administration even tried to co-opt him but soon realized that the new Venezuelan government was willing to stand up for its sovereignty and reject any type of tutelage from the United States—a fact they recognized as early as the Vargas Tragedy, the large mudslide that left a toll of nearly twenty-five thousand in 1999. By the time George W. Bush came to power in the United States, Chávez had rekindled relations with China, strengthened Venezuela's ties to Cuba, and embarked on a world tour to visit the heads of state of the Organization of Petroleum Exporting Countries (OPEC), which the United States frowned upon. In this tour, he visited places such as Iran, Saddam Hussein's Iraq, and Muammar Gaddafi's Libya. Chávez was convinced that the world needed to shift from the unipolarity that resulted from the end of the Cold War to a new multipolar world where diverse views and regional powers could emerge to give a new balance to international relations. Chávez had broken with years of Venezuelan deference to the guidance of the US State Department and began crafting his own foreign policy in terms more suitable for Venezuela's own interests.

In October 2001, after George W. Bush had divided the world between the United States and "the terrorists," Chávez spoke out against the US retaliation on Afghanistan by using the phrase: "You can't fight terrorism with more terror." Less than a year later, the United States had embarked on a regime change operation and supported a military coup against Hugo Chávez in April 2002. A coordinated effort between large Venezuelan media outlets, the business sector, parasitic labor union leaders, and disaffected sectors of the military carried out a coup against Chávez with the blessing and support of US Ambassador Charles Shapiro. This attempt only lasted forty-seven hours, only to be astonishingly overturned by a constitutionalist military and large crowds of people demanding respect for their elected leader. Later that year, an oil lockout, also backed by the US, failed to produce Chávez's ouster, only lasting two months. Rather than weaken or threaten Chávez, these attempts to undermine his government radicalized the Bolivarian Revolution, and it embarked on major transformations that included land reform, a renationalization of the oil industry towards more favorable terms for Venezuela, and the crafting of different regional integration projects with the absence of the United States.

By 2004, the United States flooded Venezuela with funds from United States Agency for International Development (USAID) and the National Endowment for Democracy (NED), aimed at promoting and winning a recall referendum against Hugo Chávez.

Among the main recipients of US political funding was Súmate, an organization led by María Corina Machado, that since then has (unsuccessfully) been engaged in discrediting the Venezuelan electoral system. *The New York Times* reported that the NED "stepped up its assistance, quadrupling its budget for Venezuela to more than $877,000." In a landslide victory and with a flawless electoral system that was even praised as "the best in the world" by former US President Jimmy Carter, the people voted for President Hugo Chávez to remain in office.

In December of that same year, he launched what would be his most audacious regional project. Together with Cuba's Fidel Castro, they created the Bolivarian Alternative of the Americas (ALBA), a project that rejected the Free Trade Area of the Americas (FTAA, or ALCA in Spanish) promoted by the United States. The defeat of this regional free trade project came as early as 2005, when in the Summit of the Americas in Mar del Plata, Argentina, leaders like Chávez and Nestor Kirchner of Argentina rejected the deal in Bush's own presence. Not only had Venezuela changed, so had the region.

By August 2004, US Ambassador William Brownfield outlined the five-point strategy for the United States Embassy's activities in Venezuela: "(1) Strengthening democratic institutions, (2) Penetrating Chávez' political base, (3) Dividing Chavismo, (4) Protecting vital US business, and (5) Isolating Chávez internationally." This would become the strategy employed against President Chávez until his passing in 2013.

When Hurricane Katrina hit New Orleans in 2005, President Chávez offered help to the hurricane victims in an unprecedented show of solidarity. The United States rejected the assistance, but Venezuela-owned Citgo Oil Corporation, an oil subsidiary with three large refineries in the United States, began to carry out its social responsibility policy of providing discounted heating oil to low-income communities in the US in places like Baltimore, Boston, the South Bronx, and even Alaska. Other social projects such as community programs and urban agriculture were also supported by Citgo's Simón Bolívar Foundation.

Chávez continued to denounce the negative role of the United States in promoting regime change operations, and in 2006 during the United Nations General Assembly, he gave a memorable speech where he called Bush, "the Devil." Later in a *Time* magazine interview, Chávez stated that it wasn't an attack on Bush but rather a counterattack: "Bush has been attacking the world, and not only with words, but with bombs." He claimed to react against "the threat of a US empire that uses the UN to justify its aggression against half of the world" and added that his intention was to "awaken US and world public opinion."

For the later part of the 2000s, President Chávez continued to decrease Venezuela's dependency on Washington. By 2007, Venezuela canceled its debt to the IMF. Meanwhile, it also began taking important measures for nationalizing key sectors of the economy, some of which had been under the control of US corporations. The electricity sector was nationalized with the acquisition of Seneca and most of the shares of Electricidad de Caracas, both previously controlled by US capital. Likewise, there is currently a process of renationalization in the oil industry and as a result, Venezuela's revenue and control of the oil projects increases. The Venezuelan government invited corporations to join oil production through joint ventures but corporations such as ExxonMobil and ConocoPhilips refused, ending their participation in Venezuela. By 2009, the government expropriated rice processing plants from Cargill because they violated national legislation controlling product prices. Then, in 2010 it nationalized eleven oil drills which had belonged to Helmerich & Payne and expropriated the bottle and glass product manufacturing plants of Owen Illinois.

US interventionism and animosity towards Chávez continued until his passing in 2013. Chávez took daring stands against US interests in his foreign policy. In December of 2008, after Bolivia had expelled the US ambassador for interference in that country's internal affairs, Chávez announced he was also expelling the US Ambassador from Venezuela in solidarity with Bolivia. Several weeks later in January 2009, Chávez announced he was breaking relations with Israel, the top US ally in Western Asia, after the Gaza Massacre. Ever since, the Zionist lobby at the US Congress has significantly increased its attacks and campaign to discredit the Bolivarian Revolution.

At the same time, the US government continued to intervene in Venezuela supporting the opposition politically and financially, as well as promoting each point of the agenda outlined by US Ambassador William Brownfield in 2004. Chávez met personally with Obama at the fifth Summit of the Americas in Trinidad and Tobago in April of 2009, and in a reply to his "let's forget the past and move on" approach, gifted him a copy of Eduardo Galeano's *The Open Veins of Latin America,* as a reminder that to really turn the page, the United States needed to recognize what it had done to the region and make amends. The recommendation was ignored when in June of that same year, President Manuel Zelaya of Honduras, a member of ALBA, was ousted with the support of then–Secretary of State Hillary Clinton. The Obama Administration sought to recover the regional influence and respect that Bush had lost, and in a couple of instances signaled willingness for a new exchange of ambassadors with Venezuela.

Towards the end of his tenure, he made some pragmatic policy shifts to try to change the correlation of forces, including reestablishing diplomatic relations with Cuba.

Venezuela, however, became a common bargaining chip for US politicians, and as the US moved forward with restoring Cuba relations and signing the Iran nuclear deal, interests in US Congress asked in return for the Obama Administration to open the door to US sanctions against Venezuela. The context had changed. Nicolás Maduro by now had been elected as Chávez's successor and misreading how profoundly committed the Venezuelan people were to the continuation of the revolutionary process, the US underestimated President Maduro's popularity and resolve.

MADURO DEEPENS THE REVOLUTION AMID ATTACKS

On March 9, 2015, Obama signed an Executive Order classifying Venezuela as an "unusual and extraordinary threat to the national security and foreign policy of the United States." This opened the door to a new series of unilateral coercive measures—which the United States wrongfully labels as "sanctions," when in fact it lacks the authority to sanction other countries. The first measures were targeting government officials announcing visa cancellations (if they had one), bank account closings (if they owned one), but above all, restraints on US persons dealing with or speaking to sanctioned individuals. This has an effect on their responsibilities in Venezuela, impacting all of the population, not just the individual. The possibility of exchanging ambassadors once again was lost, and tensions continued even though Obama even admitted in an interview that he did not consider Venezuela to be a "threat" to US national security. Meanwhile, the opposition managed to win parliamentary elections. President Maduro recognized the defeat of the revolutionary forces in those elections, and until today, the United States only formally recognizes that National Assembly elected in 2015, as Venezuela's only legitimate and democratic authority.

Donald Trump was elected in 2016, and days before leaving office, Obama renewed the executive order that allowed for sanctions on Venezuela, opening the door for Trump and his anti-Venezuelan and anti-Cuban allies to promote a "maximum pressure" campaign, a comprehensive US sanction policy that would eventually weaken Venezuelan economy, impair social transformations, co-opt the Venezuelan armed forces, and generate so much stress and suffering that the population would eventually retrieve its support from the *Chavismo* to achieve regime change. By this time, the leadership of the most extremist opposition in Venezuela decided not only to get support from the United States, but to directly take on the confrontation against the government.

From measures against key government figures, Trump expanded the attack to blockade Venezuela's oil industry, its vessels, its gold trade, its national airline, and so on. Most of the 931 measures against Venezuela to date came under the Trump Administration. His representative for the "transition" in Venezuela, Elliott Abrams, told us in a 2019 meeting that everything from food to gasoline was going to run out unless President Maduro decided to leave. A country that had an average yearly income of nearly $60 billion in 2013 could only count on an income of $710 million by 2020. Furthermore, the US-led regime change operation included the unprecedented recognition of a self-proclaimed president, Juan Guaidó, and the nonrecognition of President Maduro and the rest of Venezuela's institutions as legitimate.

Recognizing Guaidó allowed for Venezuela's foreign accounts to be frozen, Citgo Petroleum Corporation to be taken away from Petróleos de Venezuela, S.A. (PDVSA, a state-owned company), and thirty-one tons of Venezuelan gold to be taken by the Bank of England. None of these assets, together with Venezuela's $5 billion of special IMF drawing rights, were made available to the Venezuelan people during the COVID-19 pandemic. Inflation was induced by foreign distortions on the exchange rate, and migration was stimulated by a campaign in which professionals were lured to leave the country and become part of the workforce of other countries in the region. However, when the working class also started to migrate, deeper controls were established, and many Venezuelans were exposed to xenophobia and human trafficking and became victims of criminal gangs.

Both in 2014 and in 2017, street violence in the style of Color Revolutions was promoted but were eventually subdued. On August 4, 2018, explosives carried by drones almost took President Maduro's life and that of the highest-ranking officials of the Venezuelan government. Within a year of that event, there was an attempted invasion in February 2019 when dissidents disguised as humanitarian aid workers and invoking the Western concept of "Right to Protect," attempted to bring in weapons through the border with Colombia. In 2020, a group of mercenaries trained in Colombia by two US Green Berets also launched a failed military invasion; in March 2019, a sophisticated hacking operation knocked out Venezuela's power grid for several days; a military coup was attempted by Guaidó in April 2019 but lacked sufficient popular support; and in March 2020, just weeks into the COVID-19 pandemic, a $15 million reward was placed on President Maduro's head.

The US also incorporated the border controversy with Guyana, a debate which contests nearly one hundred thousand miles of territory and dates back to the times of British colonialism, into its attacks. Both countries address the territorial dispute following the Geneva Accord of 1966, which called for a peaceful and mutually satisfying solution. Although still unresolved, diplomatic contacts and attempts at solutions were put in place for decades until 2015, when ExxonMobil began to seek concessions in disputed waters. ExxonMobil's former CEO-turned-secretary of state then pressured the UN to support Guyana's unilateral decision to take the case to the International Court of Justice. Today, not only is ExxonMobil lurking in the area, but security forces linked to the Southern Command and to the Central Intelligence Agency (CIA) have also established bases, turning into another threat to Venezuelan sovereignty and regional peace.

President Maduro has fought back. Food shortages were countered with organized food distribution and subsidies through the Local Committees of Planning and Supply (CLAP) which guaranteed basic food for seven million families. An Anti-Blockade Law was designed by the Constituent Assembly to ease processes through which oil could be exported and revenues could be channeled towards social investment amidst the blockade. Actions were taken in the economic sphere to fight induced inflation and finally overcome hyperinflation and the damage done to public salaries by low state income. Nearly a million migrants were helped to return to Venezuela through the Return to the Homeland program with the state-owned (and later sanctioned!) airline, Conviasa. Food imports even managed to be substituted by national production.

The epic of the Venezuelan people and its revolutionary government during the past ten years is testament of resistance and commitment to maintaining its own independent political, social, and economic path. Despite shortcomings and difficulties, most of the Venezuelan people could point to President Maduro's government as the guarantee that people-focused policies would remain in place. Comparisons with the extreme-right debacles of the region reinforce this view. Instead, in Venezuela, the last two years have shown steady growth—the largest in Latin America according to the UN Economic Commission for Latin America and the Caribbean (ECLAC)—together with social peace and stability. The promise of positive social transformations despite current attacks was the basis for President Maduro's reelection.

When looking at the Venezuelan election of July 28, 2024, we must see it in the context of a regime change campaign of over two decades. It has never been about democracy, and it was never about the votes. Running María Corina Machado in unverifiable primaries despite knowledge of her legal prohibition to hold office was enough proof that the strategy was never electoral, but rather insurrectional. After Machado chose Edmundo González as her surrogate, it was she who did the campaigning and who remained the main figure of the extreme opposition. They needed her to carry out a manual-type fraud claim that seeks now to gather international support and generate enough internal pressure so that part of the military and parts of the working-class population would turn against the government and overthrow it. But once again, this strategy underestimated the Venezuelan people.

The insurrectional strategy required not only the narrative of alternate results giving the victory to the González–Machado candidacy, but also, the irruption of fascist violence that would terrorize Chavismo into accepting this false narrative. During the two days after the election, fascist shock groups took the streets of Venezuela and targeted thousands of United Socialist Party of Venezuela (PSUV) grassroot leaders, the military barracks and security posts, monuments, and public works built under the revolution, eventually producing twenty-five victims. This violence was in large part committed by paid criminals, of whom over 80 percent did not even vote during the election. Once the crime operation was disbanded by Venezuelan authorities, it has become evident that there is no public support for this strategy, but rather that most Venezuelans are committed to maintaining national peace. The most significant result of the violent protests of 2014 and 2017 was precisely a rejection by the majority of the Venezuelan people, regardless of their ideological positions, of any type of violence.

In November, a new president will be elected in the United States and there will be another opportunity for both countries to engage. The outlook, however, is not that hopeful. On the one hand, if the current administration's position is any indication of what a Harris government would be and she chooses to follow a Guaidó 2.0 strategy, tensions will continue for an undetermined amount of time. If, on the other hand, Trump returns to the White House without a significant change in his national security and foreign policy teams dealing with Latin America, then we can expect a new edition of the maximum pressure campaign. Venezuela, in any case, will continue its path towards socialism and a prosperous future. If ever there is a government in the White House willing to coexist with its socialist path, to engage in diplomacy, and to abandon its senseless regime change strategy, that government will find a Bolivarian Revolution willing to reestablish relations based on shared interests and mutual respect. Otherwise, it will always find Venezuela's willingness to struggle and resist, fighting to guarantee its sovereignty and life with dignity for its population.

'BEFORE THEY SEND IN THE TROOPS, THEY SEND IN THE JOURNALISTS'

BY ALAN MACLEOD

Alan MacLeod is Senior Staff Writer for MintPress News. Afvter completing his PhD in 2017, he published two books: Bad News from Venezuela: Twenty Years of Fake News and Misreporting *and* Propaganda in the Information Age: Still Manufacturing Consent. *Along with a number of academic articles, he has also contributed to* FAIR.org, The Guardian, Salon, The Grayzone, Jacobin Magazine, *and* Common Dreams.

This is a text adapted from a speech given at the "Second Meeting for a World Socialist Alternative" in Venezuela on July 23, 2024, followed by a close-reading of a Western media article on Venezuela's recent elections.

I am an investigative journalist for *MintPress News*, looking into every aspect of US foreign policy, the US military, the US and social media, and how those issues connect with each other. Before that, I was an academic, and I completed my PhD on the subject of how the Western press covers Venezuela. And after spending four years researching this topic every day and speaking to countless journalists and editors involved in Western media, I can tell you with absolute certainty that there is a media war against Venezuela being consciously fought by those in London, New York, Madrid, and Washington DC.

Venezuelans often talk about a *guerra mediatica* inside their own country, but the media war from outside is just as real. If you read the big media in the West—*The New York Times*, CNN, the BBC—they will tell you that this upcoming election is a sham, a one-sided contest presided over by a dictatorship. And yet, they will also tell you that Edmundo González is a shoo-in to win. That he is a wildly popular, father-of-the-nation character who is uniting Venezuela like a twenty-first-century Simón Bolívar. The coverage falls into the same old stereotypes as in previous elections: presenting President Maduro as a

strongman, while the opposition coalition fights a last-ditch attempt
to save Venezuelan democracy.

I think this audience, though, is well-aware that this is happening.
And so I am not going to spend my time going through example after
example of egregious media bias against your country and your government. What is more useful is to share my insights into *why* and *how*
this happens. I interviewed many of the most prominent journalists
covering Venezuela for Western media, and many of them were astonishingly frank and open with me about what they saw their role as,
and how easily they found it was to lie about Venezuela.

For example, Anatoly Kurmanaev, who works for *The New York
Times*, told me, on camera, after about ten minutes of chatting, that
he sees himself and his colleagues as "mercenaries for hire," and that
he regularly inserts false or grossly exaggerated information into
his articles in order to serve an agenda. He told me about the time
he planted a story about a single condom costing $750 in Venezuela
thanks to failed socialism. It went viral worldwide, and he described
it as a "sexy trick" he and other journalists use. Other reporters told
me that their colleagues see themselves as the shock troops in an
information war against the government of Venezuela, that they call
themselves "the resistance" to Chávez and now Maduro, and they
scheme ways to "get rid" of them.

They are, in a sense, activists posing as neutral journalists. Fran-
cisco Toro, for example, resigned from his post at *The New York
Times*, claiming that [quote], "Too much of my lifestyle is bound up
with opposition activism" that he "can't possibly be neutral." Yet Toro
was later employed by the *Washington Post* to write about Venezuela.
I also interviewed Western reporters who quietly disagreed with their
outlets' coverage, but they told me that they were forced to seriously
temper what they wrote and said that, otherwise, they knew their
bosses would not accept it. This is what Matt Kennard, who covered
Venezuela and Latin America for the *Financial Times*, told me:

> I just never even pitched stories that I knew would never
> get in. What you read in my book would just never, ever,
> in any form, even in news form, get into the *FT*. And I
> knew that, and I wasn't stupid enough to even pitch it. I
> knew it wouldn't even be considered. After I got knocked

back from pitching various articles, I just stopped. . . It was complete self-censorship.

Increasingly, Western media outlets simply outsource their Venezuela reporting to local journalists—but only those affiliated with oppositional groups. They also use "evidence" provided by opposition-aligned think tanks and NGOs, many of whom receive money from the US government through the likes of their National Endowment for Democracy. And, of course, we know what the US means by democracy. We have seen what they mean in Afghanistan, Libya, Iraq, Ukraine, and beyond. And so, the media has built up a perfect system of Western journalists citing Western-funded think tanks and NGOs, all giving them the same story they want to tell about Venezuela.

Why is this happening? The short answer is that in a capitalist system, the media are agents of the capitalist class, and they want to see the end of any attempts to build socialism in Venezuela. We like to think, in the West, of the media as brave, plucky truth-tellers standing up to power and holding it accountable. But in reality, our media is owned and dominated by billionaires. They are massive transnational corporations with their own agendas. In short, the media do not challenge power: they are power. They are the mouthpieces of the global oligarch class. And they do not take kindly to anyone or anything that challenges their power.

The United States has employed both hard power and soft power against Venezuela. Hard power in the form of sanctions and military threats: Donald Trump, let us not forget, pushed for an American invasion of Venezuela, saying it would be very "cool" if the US took over the country, because, after all, it was basically the United States anyway. But the US has also used soft power against Venezuela, trying to isolate it diplomatically, or present it as a dictatorship or a rogue state. And that is the crucial role that the corporate media play in this story.

None of this—not the sanctions, and certainly not the regime change attempts and any military action—would be at all palatable to the American public if Venezuela was not first demonized in our media. And it is that imperial role that has been so crucial to the US empire. Media constitutes an important front in the battle for Venezuela, softening up the public for regime change. Remember: before they send in the troops, they send in the journalists first.

And so, the question arises: What to do about all of this?

Well, it is crucial to fight back. To establish, support, and promote alternative media to the dominant, US-supported, oligarch-controlled media. That the United States and other Western nations have a stranglehold over our means of communication has been understood for a long time, and serious efforts to change that go back to at least 1980 with the UNESCO MacBride report. President Chávez understood this, and his government attempted to create an international TV channel to rival CNN. More attempts like these need to be tried, and with the world shifting to a more multipolar one, perhaps it is more possible than ever to do something like that.

We must not kid ourselves that social media is the answer. Those platforms are owned and controlled by Silicon Valley billionaires with close ties to the US government and the US national security state, and, at times of peak political importance, they are used against revolutionary governments. Just look at what happened to Nicaragua in 2021: just a week before the election, Facebook shut down dozens of the most important pro-Sandinista news channels in an attempt to swing the election to the pro-US candidate. And that Facebook team that carried out this censorship was full of national security officials who used to work for the CIA.

Nevertheless, those that want a fairer, better media system have to fight on every playing field, building up independent, international networks of communication, whether that is online or offline, that can disseminate information that challenges the dominant imperialistic narratives. It is not easy, but building a better world rarely is.

I always say that it is okay if changing the media is not your number one issue, but it had better be at least number two, otherwise, no one will hear your message. If we want to fight for and win a better world, changing our media system is absolutely crucial. It's not easy, but it is what has to be done.

CLOSE READING WESTERN MEDIA ON VENEZUELA

The following is adapted from a X/Twitter thread Alan MacLeod published online, that close-reads an article titled, "Choreographed Celebrations in Venezuela as Maduro Claims Win" from the BBC, published July 29, 2024, by Ione Wells. The excerpts from the BBC article are in italics, with MacLeod's emphasis in bold.

implying they're fake, artificial

Choreographed celebrations in Venezuela as Maduro claims win

"claims" rather than just "wins"

Fig. 1 | Headline of BBC article with annotations

Western media's finest propagandists are pulling out all the stops, trying to delegitimize the elections in Venezuela. In the following essay, I'll dissect their tactics, line by line, using a BBC article as an example, so you can understand how they do it.

> *As the electoral authorities, which Nicolás Maduro controls, announced he'd won a third term in office, an instant crackle of fireworks rippled around the Venezuelan Caracas.*

> *The city soundtracked in a carefully curated way, like many things in this election.*

> *The opposition claimed instantly that they, not the president, had won.*

First sentence in, and they have already poisoned the well, directly asserting that Nicolás Maduro "controls" the election, and that the whole process is "carefully curated." Second: they breathlessly repeat opposition claims of fraud, without informing readers that the opposition has claimed they have won literally every single election since 2000, yet have produced zero evidence for this, and have, every time, been proven to be lying. Not telling readers this is a crime against journalism and tantamount to incitement.

> *The opposition claimed instantly that they, not the president, had won.*

> *But you wouldn't know this from watching the news here.*

> *Television screens up and down the country only showed jubilant crowds, draped in the Venezuelan flag, dancing and cheering on the president.*

This is absolutely ludicrous. There are plenty of opposition-aligned media here. And the idea that a single person in Venezuela doesn't know that the opposition claims they won is ridiculous.

> *Nicolás Maduro does have some loyal supporters still, known as "Chavistas" after his mentor Hugo Chavez and the brand of socialism he created.*

> *But their numbers are highly disputed, and this election result is far from over.*

This phrase deliberately casts socialism as a dying, unpopular movement in Venezuela. This is probably the most blatantly egregious lie that the media tells about the country. Maduro was able to attract a massive crowd to his final pre-election rally in Caracas. Some estimates put the number as high as two million people (see Fig. 2). Maduro's supporters are as enthusiastic as they are numerous, and his final rally drew "at least five times" as many people as the opposition's final rally, according to an international election observer who spoke to me after attending both.

Fig. 2 | Pre-election rally of two million in Caracas

This is the kind of rally that a dying, unpopular figure with barely any supporters puts on, according to the BBC. I took a twenty-minute bus ride from my hotel to get to the front. The back of the rally reportedly stretched almost all the way back to the hotel.

> *As the city hums back into life this morning, the government faces pressure from both the **international community** and the opposition here to explain their numbers—after the opposition were so far ahead in the polls beforehand.*

"The international community," in mediaspeak, is a codeword for the United States and its allies, and always has been. Many countries—from regional neighbors to global powers—have already endorsed the elections.

Polls in Venezuela are notoriously bad, and many of them are directly funded and supported by the CIA, through its National Endowment for Democracy program. These US-funded polls exist to present the government as falling, and the opposition as extremely popular, in order to (1) Gin up support for US-backed candidates in Venezuelan election; (2) Give media something to cite, to make it seem like the government is about to fall, so it can bolster the "elections in Venezuela are fraudulent" narrative.

Media like the BBC regularly cite polling organizations who were off by up to sixty points during the last elections. That's akin to an American pollster confidently predicting the Green Party will sweep all fifty states. Some of these polls' methodology is laughable and are literally based on Twitter polls! Furthermore, there were plenty of polling organizations showing that Maduro was going to win comfortably—or even by a landslide. Why does the BBC never cite those ones? We know why: because it would burst their regime change narrative.

> *There are some things that are **indisputable**. Some which I, as an observer on the ground, was witness to.*

> *There were the **huge queues** at polling stations, but only tiny amounts of people being let in at one time.*

Apparently, all this, for the BBC, is "indisputable." So let's dispute it. I visited five polling stations in Caracas. Only one of them featured huge queues. The other four were running smoothly. (Interestingly, the huge lines were at a polling station in La Vega, a strongly pro-government area).

> *This led to accusations of deliberate delays, perhaps in the hope some people would give up and go home.*

> *When our **BBC team** arrived at one polling station, the organizer of the station took a call saying the international media were there. One hundred fifty people were then suddenly allowed to be admitted.*

This part sounds extremely unlikely to me. I, and other international observers with me, faced zero barriers from entering any polling stations we wanted. The reception from electoral workers ranged from amicable to polite indifference. We saw nothing out of the ordinary like this.

Interestingly, some of the polling stations were run by election officials who were openly members of the opposition. The chief of one polling station in central Caracas told me, a foreign journalist (plus observers from Zambia, Pakistan, South Africa, and the United States that I was with at the time) that she was a member of the opposition, that she strongly disliked the government, and that the country was in a shambles. Nevertheless, she said, she had complete faith in the electoral system itself.

Throughout the day, the words electoral workers we spoke to across the city used most to describe proceedings that day were "*tranquilo*" (calm) and "*fluido*" (fluid). I walked around with a camera and a tripod all day, and no one took any notice of me or any of the other foreign media I traveled with, except to welcome us, and thank us for covering the elections. This included opposition supporters, who seemed happy that we were there, and more than happy to tell us what they thought of Maduro.

> *There were allegations that some of those who work for the state, including police students, were told how to vote.*

Allegations? From whom? Nameless nobodies that the BBC could easily just have conjured from thin air.

I obviously haven't spoken to everyone in Venezuela to check, but the media have used this canard to demonize the elections in Venezuela for over twenty years, without providing much proof.

Furthermore, there have been empirical studies of this claim. For the 2013 elections, for example—Maduro's first electoral victory—the US-funded anti-Chavista organization, the Carter Center looked at this exact question, and did an anonymous survey of the Venezuelan population.

What they found was that less than 1 percent of Venezuelans report feeling pressured in any way at all to vote in a certain way. *And twice as many people reported being pressured into voting for the opposition candidate than for Maduro.[1]*

> *There was the fact President Maduro's face remained emblazoned above some poll stations even on voting day.*

> *His face lines almost every street in Caracas, with his governing party paying for incentives for people to support him—buses put on for people to attend his rallies, and free food parcels handed out.*

The idea that poor people's vote can be bought for nothing more than a parcel of food is an extremely old—and, frankly, racist—canard that goes back well over twenty years in reporting on Venezuela. I wrote an entire academic paper on the dehumanizing way in which the media dismiss working-class Venezuelans as sheep whose loyalty can be bought with nothing more than some booze or a sandwich.[2] It has its roots in the days when rich Venezuelans would openly say that poor people should not be allowed to vote.

> *Even prior to allegations of explicit fraud the question was asked: Is this contest fair?*

> *Opposition candidates were banned from running, opposition aides detained, many Venezuelans overseas struggled to register to vote and many international election observers were disinvited.*

One of the most important ways in which deceitful media can present Venezuela as a dictatorship is by providing contextless half-truths. Here is a great example. It is true that major opposition figures like Maria Corina Machado have been banned from running. But what is the context behind this ban?

---

1   "Preliminary Report: Study Mission of the Carter Center: Presidential Elections in Venezuela" (The Carter Center, April 14, 2013), https://www.cartercenter.org/resources/pdfs/news/peace_publications/election_reports/venezuela-pre-election-rpt-2013.pdf.
2   Alan MacLeod, "Chavista 'Thugs' vs. Opposition 'Civil Society': Western Media on Venezuela," *Race & Class* 60, no. 4 (April 1, 2019): 46–64, https://doi.org/10.1177/0306396818823639.

Just a few years ago, Machado went to the Organization of American States (for some reason, as a representative of Panama) and tried to organize a US-led invasion of Venezuela! She has also led waves of terroristic violence that targeted schools, hospitals, universities, public housing, and any other symbol of the collectivist society the Chavistas are trying to build. This violence has killed huge numbers of people and done billions of dollars of damage to the country. She has also attempted to organize an Israeli-led invasion of Venezuela.

In any other country, she would have spent the rest of her life in prison, if not have been executed. But in Venezuela, her primary punishment is that she can't hold office for a certain time period.

> *The international community has been divided for some time over how to respond to Venezuela, with some governments' conceding privately that the sanctions haven't "worked," either by incentivising regime change or compelling President Maduro to hold fair elections.*

> *They are also used as an excuse by President Maduro, and his supporters, for the country's woes.*

Another extremely common tactic of dishonest journalists is to present facts as accusations and accusations as facts, when it suits them. We have already seen anonymous allegations presented as pieces of hard evidence, but here we see the fact that sanctions have destroyed the country being presented merely as an "excuse" that President Maduro uses for his misrule. US government documents explicitly state that the goals of sanctions are to "bring about hunger, desperation, and overthrow of government." Anti-Venezuelan government academics in the US have calculated that US sanctions caused Venezuela to lose 99 percent of its international income. And yet the idea that sanctions are significantly to blame for Venezuela's woes is still presented by our media as a marginal conspiracy theory.

> *The future of Venezuela and whether it can rebuild matters for the rest of the world—mass emigration has fuelled a migration crisis on the US border, its vast oil reserves remain rela-*

*tively unusable, and it remains an ally for **Russia, China, Cuba and Iran** in the West.*

The opposition, meanwhile, aren't set to back down without putting up a fight.

Very often in corporate/establishment media, the most important information is in the final paragraph. And here is no exception. It explains the reason for all these lies and half-truths: Venezuela has massive oil reserves that the US wants and is an ally of many of the US' key global enemies. That is why there is such a big push right now to remove the rightful government from power. Remember: before they send in the troops, they send in the journalists first.

THE POLITICS OF ANTI-POLITICS: ORIGINS OF THE VENEZUELAN OPPOSITION

BY DIEGO SEQUERA

Diego Sequera (Caracas, 1983) is an editor, journalist, author, and researcher. He has a bachelor's degree in Literature from the Central University of Venezuela. He cofounded Misión Verdad. He was an advisor for the Venezuelan Foreign Relations Ministry, former MEP Javier Couso, and also in Agrarian Conflict Resolution.

Barely a thread in the major fabric of Venezuela's historical evolution through the last stretch of the twentieth century, this essay outlines a decisive feature of the ways that politics and the political process were exerted once the system found itself dealing with the first signs of structural crisis and as the crisis developed during the '90s.

Late '70s Venezuela, with its widespread corruption and eroding practices, became the starting point for conceiving a new way out of the general notion, established up to that point, on how the country should be run. Without a real, significant counterbalance from the left, already painfully domesticated and marginalized, the paradox of wielding politics stripped of its basic conventions versus reducing them to aesthetic means of prosecuting, achieving, and managing state power went mainstream, becoming what during the '90s was a staple word: *la antipolitica*, or the anti-politics.

It was an idea without a single point of origin. While it grew from global capitalist demand, it also came from the conquest of the state by the emergent comprador private sector which obeyed a well-established oligarchical worldview. This worldview preceded the new frameworks that became the basis for participation and enrichment, eventually impregnating the left-wing political structures becoming itself an epochal representation of "common sense." This transformation, in a way, explains why, during the heartrending '90s, the popular response to state dismantling and privatization of everything manifested from the barracks, led by mid-level, talented officer cadre instead of the usual places, on a highly historical trend that in every sense opposed the end of history.

How do we understand what we know now as "the Venezuelan opposition"? We can understand them as the myriad of names, political origins, situations, and actions that have coalesced during the Bolivarian years in different formations and groupings, to cyclically challenge the conventional paradigm of the left-right political spectrum, and at the same time, the ways to conceive popular, grassroot politics, sovereignty, and independence. By the same measure, they also highlight the highly US-dependent status of the majority of forces that led the charge against the Bolivarian Revolution. By the same measure, it also highlights the highly US-dependent status of the majority of forces that led the charge against the Bolivarian Revolution.

The cycle of armed struggle for national liberation in Venezuela came to an early end (compared to the rest of the region). The military defeat of the left, after an intense (large-scale) six-year counterinsurgency war, gave rise to three things: formal pacification, the residual persecution of the remaining resistance pockets (which would last for decades), and the dispersal due to the defeat of the parties that led the struggle. This trauma and degradation stripped away each of their chances of becoming a political option from the moment they were legally allowed to participate in the 1973 elections.

The essentially bipartisan consensus of the Punto Fijo Pact could now proceed without major obstacles. The "democratic game" manifested between the social-democratic option (Acción Democrática—AD, from here on) and the Christian-democratic one (the Comité de Organización Política Electoral Independiente—Copei, from now on), operating freely.

THE ORIGINS OF ANTI-POLITICS AND VENEZUELAN MANAGERIALISM (1958-1998)

In the 1970s, as the United States recovered from Vietnam and the OPEC crisis, Venezuela adjusted to a new world order, aligning itself with the dollar and beginning to modify the ways it interacted with other countries. Venezuela "nationalized" its oil, moving from being a lackey to a "partner." The country created a middle class, leaving only crumbs behind, all while ensuring that the oligarchy was not threatened and that oil revenues paid for everything.

The Saudi-brokered peace was showing all the signs of its unsustainability and short-termism. The enormous sums of money facilitated new schemes of criminal accumulation that spread throughout the entire Venezuelan state apparatus. Politically, during the 1980s, the distinction between the state and the government was completely erased. The ruling party controlled the entire structure of the executive branch in the country and the central government. Frictions increased. Every single economic sector depended, in different ways, on the hypertrophied petro-state: Venezuela's secular rentier economy.

Fiscal distortions worsened, the imbalance of power grew, and the Punto Fijo model was eroded entirely. The dynamics of this deformed and dependent single-product economy made the nation's vulnerabilities increasingly visible in the face of the "new" conditions of the international system. The private sector, despite benefiting from state revenues, became more exposed to the influence of Wall Street and the City (London's financial district), and began to move faster than the political sectors.

❖ ❖ ❖ ❖ ❖

From the beginning of "democracy" in 1958, each political structure was inevitably accompanied by a representative from the economic-business sector. By the mid-1970s, a proper managerial class gradually began to emerge.

In the absence of any real counterbalance from the left in any of its forms, the challenge to the state came from the opposite side. Faced with gradual decomposition, moral degradation, and other symptoms, the oligarchic-managerial sectors were becoming increasingly self-aware and conscious of their alleged role in society. Over the late 1970s, two groups—half-think-tank, half-lobby—made up of experts, academics, expansive business oligopolies, banks, and media owners, gained the capacity to exert pressure outside of the party system.

The Roraima and Santa Lucía Groups organized meetings and conferences, published communiqués, wrote in newspaper columns, and increasingly dominated radio and television airtime. They were forging the notion that they were a group destined to take the reins of the nation, gestating and refining the key line of their discourse: the country's main problem was the political class and its relationship with a mammoth state which was completely paralyzed and capturing the oil and iron income. It was a moral problem but, most importantly (as logic dictated), a problem of administration.

It was increasingly evident (they argued), that career politicians and their parties were incapable of managing the country's massive publicly owned enterprises (telecommunications, the postal system, basic industries, construction projects, the transportation system, and—God forgive us—the oil industry). Three decades of stagnant neo-Keynesianism had proven that the country needed a major shift (pun intended), and this could not be executed by the Punto Fijo Pact.

From the banks, certain industries, and other historic commercial sectors, this vision was echoed, but one group stood out above the rest.

Marcel Granier and Peter Bottome were the main leaders of 1BC (One Broadcasting Corporation), the parent company of Radio Caracas Televisión (RCTV), Radio Caracas Radio, and El Diario de Caracas. Granier was the most visible and active figure of the Roraima Group (Moisés Naím would be the epitome of the Santa Lucía Group). Both were indirect heirs of the vast power of the Phelps family, a recent dynasty from the United States—but not one of the grand colonial and nineteenth-century surnames. The Phelps family had gradually displaced German trading houses in the 1900s to position themselves as a key force in importing US goods, as pioneers in the mass communication business, and as reference names in the scientific field (particularly ornithology), culture, and the new high society that expanded along with oil contracts and the state's soft loans. But Granier was not part of the genetic inheritance. He became an heir by marrying one of the daughters of the Phelps patriarch, William H. Phelps Jr. On the other hand, Bottome was the son of the Venezuelan-American's second wife—an heir in the second degree.

Another major oligopolistic figure (and rival to these two), Gustavo Cisneros, also married another daughter of Phelps and represented the other oligopolistic force, working closer and more directly with the governments since the 1970s. Through his organization, the Cisneros Group, he also established a television network (Venevisión) and bought a large portion of Nelson Rockefeller's commercial chain in the country. Granier's rise, compared to Cisneros, followed a different path: Cisneros enjoyed systematic and privileged relationships with the government since 1974. Like Bottome, he was not only a media entrepreneur, but also a representative of the US arms industry, acting as the liaison between General Dynamics (the F-16 aircraft manufacturer) and the Venezuelan government.

Through the media, Granier simultaneously attacked the state and pressured those who opposed his business interests. His ambition was marked by opportunism, as he did not belong to the highest historic caste, and he had to violently forge his place. If RCTV was his elite unit, his Sunday interviews, the actions of the Roraima Group, and his preaching against the state were his infantry. And his roadmap was a book published under his name, *The Omnipotent State vs. the Next Generation* (1984), though legend has it that the Argentine writer Tomás Eloy Martínez was the ghostwriter. The title of "his work" clearly established the frontline of his war.

Granier's influence shaped the behavior of the groups that would follow, now much more absorbed into the logic of finance and neoliberalism: promoters of that new common sense of the era. They were at the forefront of the campaign against the establishment, the promoters of a trend that would turn the page of history. Their preaching and struggle were framed under the concept that would become crucial: in opposition to the politics of politicians, there was anti-politics.

As these groups spread dissent, demonstrating their firepower and reach through mass radio and television broadcasts (and supporting their hidden aspirations for total power and protection of their interests), there lay a backdrop of legitimate and indisputable social unrest. Venezuela, stuck and stagnant, had suffered from the betrayal of ideals and the failure to fulfill every promise of prosperity. Hunger, malnutrition, unemployment, repression, and police abuse; the obscene corruption across all branches of power; childhood uncertainty, family degradation, the territorial saturation of poverty in large slums, rural depopulation, and general dysfunction—all were real and affected almost the entire population, including the now equally battered national middle class, which had come close to touching the contours of the illusion of a better future. By 1988, the general sentiment of "enough is enough," the frustration that came with it, was fully imbued in the people, and the social temperature was just one degree from boiling.

✵✵✵✵✵

By 1988, everything was systemically demanding a shift towards the new metabolism of capital, the one advocated by Roraima and Santa Lucía, with the party structures and the public sphere at their limit. The media overexposed extreme poverty and the rosy lives of the upper echelons of society. The advertising revolution was wreaking havoc.

It was at this moment that Carlos Andrés Pérez (CAP) was elected for the second time in history. The big changes, he said, were unavoidable. The system could and had to be saved. CAP was the great reformer, the Venezuelan counterpart to the great social-democratic titans of the world. He had genuinely won with popular support.

He was convinced he was going to prepare Venezuela for the twenty-first century. He had the stature to do it. To that end, he began his own perestroika and glasnost. Faced with structural stagnation, state power needed to be decentralized and regionalized—regional leaders had to become positions of popular and direct election. In the economy and finance, the world demanded a shock treatment.

❋ ❋ ❋ ❋ ❋

The state had to modernize and update its management methods. The "cleansing" of the economy, finances, and taxation required the universal prescription of the time, the magic words: structural reform.

Believing this was the cure for the ailment, CAP decided to create a cabinet that included a prominent role for the healers of the moment: this was the entry of the new managerial class into formal political power. They had all the necessary academic credentials and were largely without partisan backgrounds, "independent," representing a new breed both for the establishment and for the overwhelming majority of the population.

CAP also assembled a cabinet that included a healthy dose of career politicians, thoroughbreds who comprised the other wing of the executive branch. But political decisions rested entirely on technocratic recommendations: the restructuring of the state and the economy had to be done immediately, and the need to explain the logic behind the monumental regime of transformations the country was about to undergo was completely disregarded.

For the managerial class, there was no need for a public educational process to socialize the reforms amongst the people. They assured them that the example itself would offer all the explanations because everything would be better: it was enough to set out on the highway to the end of history. And this was the vision CAP adopted, without using his public stature to prepare society. There was no psychological preparation of the public or compensatory measures for the impact that the restructuring would have. As the expert class insisted: the human cost would be compensated by the utopian prosperity that would automatically come from the "revitalization" of politics and the economy in accordance with the new standards of the First World.

But by overlooking this pedagogical process, CAP's government created an opportunity for the anti-political movement to exacerbate the emotional side of these changes. RCTV managed to capture the zeitgeist, seeking to voraciously capitalize on it.

The first reforms were implemented just as the new government took office in February. But this reality was out of touch with the people. The front pages of newspapers on February 27, 1989, were filled with bold headlines about the bitter wedding of an aristocratic family, along with endless pages promoting a whole range of products, both necessary and superfluous, that were absolutely out of reach for more than three-quarters of the national population. This was accompanied by widespread news of the increase in gasoline prices and, consequently, public transportation fares. And then the *Caracazo* happened.

✿ ✿ ✿ ✿ ✿

The Caracazo was a popular explosion which reached an insurrectional and chaotic profile, primarily aimed not at the centers of power, but at the storefronts that embodied the division between those two seemingly different national realities. The looting of stores was an assault on goods. No political sector could anticipate the explosion, nor draw adequate lessons—at least, ones that would benefit the majority instead of serving their own calculations.

The disturbances occurred amidst the stammering of the entire left. Repression was inevitable, and repressed it was. March 1989 began with a shocking toll of the dead, detained, and disappeared, as well as businesses destroyed in the major cities of the country. The repression managed to contain the revolt, but the system had been compromised.

The first insurrection against neoliberal orthodoxy in Latin America, if not in the world, didn't immediately produce a political outcome. But its main effects were just around the corner. Meanwhile, both CAP and the managerial class continued moving forward, but not without friction. Despite everything that was said later, Pérez neither considered himself a neoliberal nor did he look favorably on the privatization of strategic public companies (his mission was to restore the greatness he had brought to the country in the '70s during the Saudi phase). But eventually, he yielded to the experts, and the privatizations began.

Members of the Roraima and Santa Lucía groups (Gustavo Roosen and Eduardo Quintero from the former, Naím from the latter) set the standards in all macroeconomic planning forums: the investment program, meetings with the IMF, negotiations to join the General Agreement on Tariffs and Trade (GATT), and the privatizations. But they never reached the point of acceleration, as the sociopolitical landscape prevented it.

Decentralization and the new forms of bidding with the government/state affected the system of interests of AD, now in open opposition to CAP. The measures sent shockwaves throughout society, earning even more widespread rejection. Quickly, CAP came to represent everything wrong with the country.

At that point, the anti-political consensus was reinforced, for various reasons, by the majority of the social spectrum. Attacks from all fronts controlled by 1BC intensified, especially on television. A comedy show, *Radio Rochela*, satirized the political establishment while slipping in the anti-political and anti-state message. Just a month after the first military uprising, a telenovela galvanized this general spirit with a clear anti-political undertone. It was called *Por estas calles*.

By 1992, Pérez's government was deeply affected by the silent war and had even retreated from its initial grand proposal, trying to appease the party system, especially AD. The siege had reached its widest scope and began closing in on Miraflores.

Discontent within the military establishment became visible, with various currents on both the left and the right. Some were bona fide forces seeking political transformation, others were opportunistic commands seizing on the situation. The best organized and most developed one, which posed an imminent danger, was forced to move earlier than planned after being discovered, advancing the operation date: February 4.

That morning, a group of mid-level officers (lieutenant colonels, majors, captains, and lieutenants) and high-ranking commanding troops rose up in the main cities of the country. The night before, CAP had returned from none other than Davos. The uprising, very close to succeeding, was defeated that day. By midday, the head of the insurrection addressed the country, took full responsibility, called for surrender, and declared that, unfortunately, the objectives were not achieved—*for now*. The emergence of this political-military movement, defining itself primarily as Bolivarian (a deeply significant and unifying code), denounced, more from the left and with a marked nationalist-populist character, the untenable nature of the situation.

As many still remember, the act of taking full responsibility for his actions, in a country resigned to seeing no one held accountable for their public and private misdeeds, earned overwhelming social sympathy, from the bottom up. But while popular aspirations were manifested in that coup, the elite sectors also found a new battering ram and point of support in destabilizing Pérez's government. A familiar but, at that point, unaccustomed pattern emerged in the Venezuelan political power imagination: someone else had conveniently done the dirty work for you.

Immediately after February 4, the technical state of insurrection across all political sectors (joined by the military and judiciary) was total. The debates in both chambers of parliament, what was said in RCTV interviews, and what was discussed on the streets sublimated into *Por estas calles* and *Radio Rochela*: everything had to change completely. Pérez was the main and sole culprit for the crisis and he had to go.

CAP ceded ground, and the managerial class of the time maneuvered less and less. At the end of that year, with the first regional elections looming, a second military uprising, from the same movement but now involving the Air Force, the Metropolitan Police, and a civilian wing, erupted on November 27.

If the uprisings reinforced the consensus across sectors of society, the attempt to hijack and operationalize of the spirit of the moment came from above. A new path was forming, one which was central and had deep approval, and was envisioned by the most advanced sectors of the consensus: a National Constituent Assembly. Even CAP was not immune to this discussion. But this entailed a significant radicalism for the multifacted conspiracy brewing in political corners: everything had to be done, but not too much. This idea of a Constituent Assembly was already too much, especially considering that the approval came from the lower classes.

The attempts to overthrow Carlos Andrés Pérez through armed force did not receive categorical rejection from the entire establishment. In fact, figures like Rafael Caldera, the pope of Copei, who now as a senator was acting independently of the party he founded, condemned the coup but emphasized the circumstances under which it took place. Meanwhile, the plan to eliminate Pérez prospered from the right.

The year 1993 began with corruption allegations magnified (and cherry-picked) from the vast repertoire of widespread corrupt practices, from which even the anti-political factions were not exempt. But one case that would transcend and garner more attention than all the others, facilitated by the 1BC–Roraima group: the infamous "secret fund." Initially reported in print media and presented to the attorney general, the parliament immediately echoed the news. The CAP government had allocated $250 million to support Violeta Chamorro in Nicaragua, supporting the security service that Pérez provided by deploying a group of forty elite officers from the Metropolitan Police (the CETA group) to serve as the security ring for the reelected Nicaraguan president. The president, who had supported and financed the Sandinista National Liberation Front during his first term, later supported the candidate of the "transition" from Sandinismo. It was for this allocation of public funds that Pérez would be tried.

Weeks later, Carlos Andrés Pérez was overthrown by the accumulation of general consensus executed by the right. Under the pretext of this flimsy and legally debatable case, the combination of political parties, the educated segments of society, and the most important faction of the economic, media, and financial elite, ousted the president a few months before he was set to legally hand over power in elections. This ousting, seen through today's lens, could be understood as proto-lawfare.

Alongside the participation of new parties in the executive, numerous initiatives from the middle class were crystallizing through a neighborhood movement that, to a large extent, allowed these sectors to engage in social participation outside of the political parties. An indirect legacy of the Causa R party (originally the most innovative left-wing group), the first wave of dispersal of traditional parties facilitated the participation of professional sectors, openly apolitical, who began to influence and, to some extent, shape local public policies. But even more importantly, they discovered a previously unknown political agency, which had irreconcilable and deep differences with grassroots and working-class organizing structures.

These were "civic" movements for themselves, but they still shared the vision of the mega-consensus. These were the first steps toward an acceptable civil society for the establishment and security agencies, but their anti-communist and pro-reform stance made it impossible to view them as a subversive force; in addition, they were part of certain links in the economic chain.

❊ ❊ ❊ ❊ ❊

In another equally telling move, Rafael Caldera, the other living pope of politics, was elected after the seven-month interim government of Ramón J. Velázquez. This was supposed to be the moment for the disparate movement that had ousted Peréz. But Caldera did not win with the support of Copei, which had its own candidate, an unquestionable representative of the most aggressive anti-political groups. AD fielded Claudio Fermín, a candidate who had benefited from decentralization, while Andrés Velázquez, promising to garner the most votes, drew support from a sector of neighborhood movements and the strictly popular vote. But Caldera won with a coalition of parties around his new group, Convergencia, supported by, among others, the Movement Towards Socialism (MAS) and the Communist Party in a sort of last-minute "historic pact."

Without the scapegoat of CAP, the game was closed: the only players left to blame were those among the general complicity of the entire party system and the now more factual powers than before. New representatives of the managerial class continued on the same path as before, colored by the appointment from the left of Teodoro Petkoff to the Ministry of Planning (Cordiplan). The Ministry looked to continue implementing the orthodox agenda (the Venezuela Agenda), now better publicized and softened, but no less aggressive in its privatization efforts, external debt, fiscal problems, and moral crisis.

But in addition to the situation worsened by wealth accumulation, the attempts to "clean up" the economy were compounded by a seismic banking crisis. The insolvency of the banking system, led by the largest conglomerate, Grupo Latino, triggered a bank run that forced the state to save what it could of the financial system. Savers were left adrift, unattended. But this also allowed the permitted flight of around fifty bankers abroad, taking with them a significant portion of the funds. And this time, they didn't have Peréz as the scapegoat; the system was at a dead end.

The era of anti-politics was being co-opted by a combination of intellectual dishonesty, systematic protection of white-collar theft, and arrogance. The weight and passage of time caught up with Caldera in the presidential seat, and by the final stage of his term, it was clear that more than Caldera, it was a small group led by two of his sons and the economic-financial power that was governing.

❋ ❋ ❋ ❋ ❋

The sustained rise of Chávez in the polls during the 1998 elections sent the rest of the system into a panic. Chávez was the only true outsider in every sense of the word. Just months before election day, all political forces threw their weight behind Salas Römer as the only credible option to preserve the system's order. The classist interpretation was unavoidable: a landowner, industrialist, and representative of the very patrician Carabobo oligarchy faced off against the retired military officer and his popular platform. The Commander's victory marked the definitive collapse of the system, which had already started to unravel during the campaign.

Thus, through the ballot box, the Bolivarian Revolution began. For the traditional political forces and the various economic power groups surrounding them, the outlook was bleak. The main bipartite formations barely survived extinction. The initiative of the strange composite of consensus represented by Caldera came too late, squandering any expectations in less than five years and confirming the inability of anti-politics to do precisely that: politics. The pressure to preserve channels of cushy jobs, control, and influence over the economic map and established culture subjected them to a credibility crisis that, even today, despite everything, persists.

*****

Some of these power circuits, true to their instincts and approach to the levers of power, harbored some hope of controlling and directing the Chávez phenomenon, but gradually it became clear that this hope was an impossible one.

When the Commander was sworn in as president under the "dying" 1961 Constitution, guaranteeing and later fulfilling his promise of a Constituent Assembly, there was little left of the old order. By 2001, in part due to the opposition he faced from the legislature, he launched the enabling laws (especially the land and hydrocarbons laws), becoming a true threat to the traditional order.

The Venezuelan national emergency at the close of the century was fundamentally caused by the erosion of the system that had emerged in 1958, but it was the hubris of the ruling class that ultimately crashed it. Starting in 1993, when the factual powers essentially faced no obstructions and, therefore, could no longer hide their parasitic, criminal, and complicit nature, they sealed their fate with the banking crisis. In a supreme irony, the slogan of the financial group at the center of the economic and moral collapse boldly stated, "the generation of those who know what they are doing."

Dispersed and affected, that same generation, and their children, would lead—using methods similar to those employed against Carlos Andrés Pérez—the extra-political and forceful ways to resist the new, insolent popular government. For this, they had different layers of sociological sediment to rely on. In the face of the near-total collapse of traditional politics (which was gradually being reconstituted), the government may no longer have been in their hands, but the overwhelming economic and media power, as well as the international contacts of the anti-political sectors, remained their main instruments of "resistance."

They also had sectors of the military and security agencies from the old regime, control of the main municipalities in eastern Caracas, key governorships (Miranda and Carabobo), and the managerial and technocratic caste that still occupied strategic positions (like PDVSA, which was close to being fully privatized). They also held sway over a significant portion of the terrified middle and professional classes—direct victims of the banking run—who harbored a deep fear of poverty and the popular classes, and who, with a deeply ingrained anti-communist mindset, were unable to see what reality was saying. This was the beginning of the era in which they would become the opposition, despite still, to this day, acting and speaking as if they were the government and in power.

THE CREATION OF (PRIVATIZED) CIVIL SOCIETY (1999-2006)

From 1999 to 2002, class instincts were on high alert in response to the tension provoked by "the process," as the revolution was popularly referred to in its early days. By popular mandate, the main demand of Chávez's campaign program—the Constituent Assembly—was being executed.

The creation of five branches of government, inspired by the Bolivarian state model outlined in the Congress of Angostura in 1819; the unification of the two chambers of the legislature into a single National Assembly; the declaration of the Republic, now Bolivarian; and the preamble of the Constitution, which declared Venezuela a "participatory and protagonist" democracy within the framework of a social state governed by law and justice, sent shockwaves throughout the country.

The dispersion of the historical party system (both on the right and the left) allowed the vacuum to be filled by a vast constellation of civil associations which, in many cases, barely concealed their oligarchic, comprador, and consular profile—it would be difficult to call them a full-fledged bourgeoisie, given the inherent levels of parasitism. This resulted in two trends. The first was the legal step toward the creation of formal parties, and the second, the increased civic nature of organizations that moved toward the path of becoming NGOs. The most complete representative of the former was the party Primero Justicia (PJ).

PJ had existed as an association since 1992. It had infiltrated the municipal administration following decentralization (in the wealthy and middle-class areas of eastern Caracas) as mediators and promoters of peace judges. With the arrival of Chavismo, the civil association Primero Justicia decided, in the year 2000, to take the step towards formalization, first as a regional party and then as a national one. The initial roster would become a who's who of the new political class emerging from the depths of anti-politics and oligarchic sectors. Julio Borges, a leader of PJ, was the main character and TV judge of *Justicia para todos* (Justice for All), a television program that settled social or family disputes (and miserably exposed domestic cases, when they were not fabricated).

Apart from Borges, the leading figures included Leopoldo López, Henrique Capriles Radonski, and Gerardo Blyde. The transition from association to party was financed by irregularly diverted funds from PDVSA by Leopoldo López's mother, marking the birth of the party with a legacy of administrative corruption and political nepotism. Nevertheless, they presented themselves as a renewing force in the landscape, representatives of the wealthy classes and the anxiously fearful middle class of the large cities. In 2000, they secured five seats in the National Assembly and won the mayorships of the municipalities of Baruta, with Capriles, and Chacao, with López.

Until the mid-1990s, Venezuela did not have what is conventionally understood today as civil society. Certainly, since the '80s, there were organizations beginning to advocate for human rights, but inevitably, being opposition to the established political order, they were marginal movements. This changed with the rise of neighborhood movements and widespread rejection of the party system of the '90s. While Primero Justicia was emerging on one side, the civic movement (associations and union bodies that would later become NGOs) was advancing separately. From this line emerged María Corina Machado and Carlos Vecchio. The former, an heir to notable surnames (Machado, Parisca, Zuloaga) and from a family linked to the steel and automotive industries; the latter from the rural bourgeoisie, who would eventually transition from civic activist to attorney for ExxonMobil in Venezuela to party leader. However, PJ's worldview was generally in line with the associations.

For them, Chávez represented a glitch in history, an accident that
allowed the long-neglected population to feel represented in government. Within this perspective, the problem was never the privatizations, nor the opening of floodgates to neoliberal globalization, nor
the hegemonic power of the United States and Europe. Rather, the
fault fell on an "incompetent" class of politicians and thieves who
allowed power to slip from their hands and fall, now, into the hands
of alleged newcomers with the ominous influence of Fidel Castro.
They claimed it was a crypto-communist movement that was merely
waiting for the opportunity to make nationalizations, abolish private
property, and "indoctrinate our children."

This, and nothing else, was what the "barefoot" government
was distilled to: representatives of a disenchanted Venezuela. To a
large extent, the *weltanschauung* (worldview) of anti-politics remained
intact, and this new generation was ready to take the reins of what, by
the law of life, belonged to them, the true heirs of "decent Venezuela."

The successive large-scale electoral failures led them to look to,
without many reservations, the only available alternatives capable of
turning the tide and avoiding the worst: the mechanisms of force.
What the parties were no longer capable of doing would be accom-
plished by the concentrated capital of economic, financial, and media
groups, alongside the (now privatized) civil society. In this way, PJ,
represented by its two mayors from Caracas, played an instrumental
role by leveraging their respective police forces and street actions to
contribute to the coup of April 2002. The brief stay of Pedro Carmona
Estanga in Miraflores left a historical document identifying the key
players in the coup and last-minute accomplices who signed the decree
dissolving the powers of the state, abolishing the constitution, and
proscribing the legitimately elected government. The popular and
military counter-coup, forty-seven hours later, saw them making one
of the most embarrassing retreats after consciously supporting a day
that inevitably demanded casualties in front of the cameras, not only
among Chavistas but also among their own supporters.

The first predominantly media-driven coup in Venezuelan history
represented anti-politics at its maximum expression up to that point.
Its main immediate effect on the government, aside from seeking for-
giveness, was defensive radicalization.

In addition to the enabling laws, another trigger for the coup was the restructuring of PDVSA, with Chávez firing the managerial class of the oil industry live on television, an act perceived as anathema. Months later after the coup was defeated, actors from the historical party system, the emerging PJ, other splinter groups from AD (like Un Nuevo Tiempo, or UNT, and Alianza Bravo Pueblo), civil associations, and powerful factions rallied under the umbrella of the Coordinadora Democrática. They aligned with the decisions made by preexisting structures that still held some power and influence, notably the Central de Trabajadores Venezolanos (CTV) and a new civil association called Gente del Petróleo, which concentrated technocratic and professional leaders expelled from PDVSA.

Beginning in 2003, with the country facing deep economic damage and nearing general paralysis, the business and oil strike began to dissolve, leading to a new moment of Chavista radicalization: the launch of major social missions broadened its support base.

In March of that same year, a delegation from the Albert Einstein Institution, led by former military officer Robert Helvey and close associate of Gene Sharp, met with various civil organizations. From those discussions emerged what would become the new tactic to finally expel Chávez from power. The constitution, which had been destroyed and publicly shunned by anti-Chavista forces until that moment, suddenly took on a new appeal, as its Article 72 offered a mechanism to enable and call for a recall referendum after half of the constitutional term had been fulfilled. In this direction, the Coordinadora Democrática and other non-partisan organizations concentrated their efforts.

To achieve this, it was necessary to gather signatures that would reach half of the registered electoral roll. At this point, an NGO focused on electoral "transparency," Súmate, founded by María Corina Machado and Alberto Plaz, a former executive of US financial consulting firm McKinsey & Co., emerged as the key organizer of the *firmazo*, the signature collection drive that would enable the referendum. However, the collection was done outside the legal deadline (before half of the term had been fulfilled, which was still months away), and it later presented millions of forged and irregular signatures.

Thus, the first *firmazo* was reversed. The scrutiny of the initial signatures provoked a reaction of street violence in the wealthy and middle-class areas of Caracas and other cities, allegedly employing "nonviolent" mechanisms to politically challenge the state and attack its sources of power. By the end of February and March 2004, Venezuela experienced its first *guarimba* in history, and once again, mayors Capriles and López were depicted front and center.

Similarly, a new signature collection drive, the *reafirmazo*, was accepted by the National Electoral Council (CNE), the electoral power, and by August, the elections were held. Essentially, the referendum asked whether the respondent agreed with President Chávez's removal. The Coordinadora Democrática launched an overwhelming and frenetic campaign for "Yes." However, the "No" won decisively. Months earlier, the Commander had declared the anti-imperialist nature of the Bolivarian Revolution.

This new political and electoral defeat plunged the "civic" sectors of the opposition into melancholy. In 2005, they attempted to boycott the parliamentary elections without success: the legislative power became one hundred percent controlled by Chavismo. In 2006, in a new attempt in the presidential elections, they were dramatically defeated by Chávez once again.

Indiscriminate massacres of both Chavistas and opponents by snipers; an induced economic paralysis attacking the oil industry on all fronts; street confrontation actions that would later become the method of choice; the arrival of Colombian paramilitary groups in association with retrograde military sectors expelled for their participation in the 2002 coup—all failed to achieve their objective. If anything, this accumulation of failures further fueled rejection and skepticism regarding a possible political or violent extra-political exit that could realign the country to its "natural state."

INDISPENSABLE UPDATES (2007-2013)

With the legitimacy of the votes, 2007 began with a Chávez who had made social advances, and a government that, while raising the quality of life for the majority of the population—leveraging a cycle of high commodity prices (particularly oil)—was able to strengthen itself economically and expand the field of structural transformations in society and the state. On the other hand, the crisis of the opposition, its inability to fully reinvent itself and effectively measure itself against Chavismo through political means, forced them to reassess and seek new ways to renew and update themselves to the undeniable keys of the Venezuelan historical context of that time.

A new high-voltage battle loomed on the horizon. RCTV was the most powerful and destructively bellicose focus of the dispersed opposition, the most effective vehicle for Granier, the Roraima Group, and anti-politics—the central engine of the 2002 coup. It also had to face the process of renewing its license in the radio spectrum, a license that had always been granted by the Venezuelan state. The difference was that what had previously been a mere formality now required accountability for its role as a battering ram in each coup attempt, for exacerbating tensions through the constant promotion of fake news, and for the psychological molding it imposed on its captive audience. With the political landscape largely cleared by the anemia of the opposition up to that point, the revolutionary government decided not to renew the concession, delivering a blow whose magnitude must be understood by looking back over the twenty years of history in the twentieth century.

It wasn't exactly official, but this seemed to have been the catalyst of a new phenomenon that would become the new "miracle," the new silver bullet with which the rapid path to neoliberal restoration would begin. Weeks before the end of RCTV's license, a new student movement emerged that, due to its apparent novelty, sparked widespread euphoria. However, the "purity" of the phenomenon was scrutinized, and the inorganic nature of the "movement" became evident.

A new phase of astroturfing began in 2007. These student groups emerged from a legacy of US and capitalist funded insurrection movements. Since 2005, they had been trained by CANVAS, the regime-change organization whose founder, Srdja Popovic, had emerged from OTPOR! (Resistance), the movement that played a key role in the ousting of Yugoslav president Slobodan Milosevic. As is well known, the overthrow of Milosevic in 2000 triggered a proliferation of these lab-engineered "revolutions" in the former Soviet orbit, employing the "nonviolent" methods of Sharp and the Albert Einstein Institute, with additional funding and training provided by the National Endowment for Democracy (NED), the US Agency for International Development (USAID), and Open Society Foundations. It is worth noting that the NGO culture had already undergone an initial phase of preparation and shaping with the USAID Office of Initiatives for Transition, which operated from 2001 to 2004. This was a higher phase, as these mechanisms that had proven effective in Eastern Europe and Central Asia became new elements on the political landscape in Venezuela.

Within this laboratory grouping, new names began to emerge, such as Freddy Guevara, David Smolansky, Yon Goicoechea, Nixon Moreno, Stalin González, and in a secondary role, Juan Guaidó. Indeed, the Bolivarian Revolution failed to successfully consolidate itself on campuses, despite having student leaders who would later participate in formal power. Regardless, the apparent "novelty" of the students following the initial stir ironically did not reveal anything new about their political vision, their tactics, their symbolic/ intellectual production, or their relationship with the generation that immediately preceded them. The anti-establishment aesthetic and the fetishization of the new were entirely compromised: it became clear that they did not represent a break from the past, but rather a perpetuation of those interests, that vision, and their essential postulates (if they can be called that), once again lacking popular content as is true across the elite opposition.

When the constitutional reform proposed by the Commander to accelerate the country toward socialism was defeated in December 2007, it marked the first electoral defeat for Chavismo by a dramatically slim margin. Although attributed to the "eruption" of "students," the electoral setback cannot be fully explained by that measure. A significant factor was the revision and articulation introduced by the National Assembly, the difficulty in explaining the breadth and detail of the reform, and even the distancing of purist left elements. Gradually, the first line of "students" entered conventional politics, leaving behind their supposed oppositional character without any contradiction in the process. A first wave did so by enrolling in PJ and UNT.

By 2006, the demand for new parties, prematurely stagnated, to update themselves and, above all, to blend in with the elements of the new political zeitgeist was undeniable. One of the first transformations occurred that same year, with Leopoldo López and Gerardo Blyde migrating to UNT, accompanied by an internal split within PJ itself, with a faction promoting itself as "popular PJ." Copei transformed into Copei–Partido Popular in a maneuver that, more than a nod, represented almost total subordination to the Spanish Partido Popular (PP). AD had restructured itself and reversed the process of disappearance.

The Coordinadora Democrática was left in ruins, and in its place, the Mesa de Unidad Democrática (MUD) arose as an umbrella for opposition parties. A first positive effect was seen with their unambiguous participation in the regional elections of 2008, where they managed to capture significant positions in the most populated states and cities. However, the "internal debate" (if it can be called that) continued, especially regarding the upcoming parliamentary elections of 2010. The MUD organized its first "primary elections" for the unitary selection of candidates. From then on, all processes of "primaries," whether assisted by the CNE or not, would never be technically and objectively scrutinized, and the grievances and discontent of some excluded actors would dissolve into the daily grind, without sufficient exposure in the "allied" media.

In 2009–2010, López had already abandoned the UNT ship. He needed a movement tailored to him. In his first phase, outside any party, he launched the so-called popular networks, an attempt to approach, infiltrate, and co-opt community initiatives in neighborhoods aligned with Chavismo. By then, he had significant funding from USAID, which was disbursed directly to leaders without going through nominal channels. The result was the incorporation of many representatives from NGOs and civil associations into the roster of leaders who would soon form the party Voluntad Popular (VP), including Carlos Vecchio and Tamara Adrián, who aimed to participate in the 2010 parliamentary elections. VP was registered with the Socialist International.

Several "students," now weathered politicians, joined VP, wielding their youthful fetish as just another element of their public discourse. Among them were Freddy Guevara, Juan Andrés Mejías, Gaby Arellano, and Juan Guaidó. López, still disqualified due to corruption charges during his tenure as mayor, could not aspire to an elected position. María Corina Machado also decided to resign from Súmate and transition from the "civil" and NGO universe to compete as an independent, first in the 2010 parliamentary primaries, and then to win a seat representing the affluent municipalities of eastern Caracas,

located in the state of Miranda. To a large extent, the formal land-
scape of parties, with the return of AD and Copei, the emergence of
VP and PJ, and the increasing distancing of the PCV from the Polo
Patriótico, was established.

The following year in 2011, the Commander announced he had
been diagnosed with cancer. With cancer weighing on him, he prepared to fight the 2012 elections.

Once again, through "primaries," it was decided who would be
the candidate of "unity." With López sidelined from the race and
Machado lacking the numbers, Henrique Capriles secured the candidacy (supported by López). Capriles, now the standard-bearer for the
motley crew representing the opposition, was defeated by more than
a million votes by the Commander in October. In December, Chávez
announced he would travel to Cuba to continue his treatment (it was
privately known that his condition was delicate), and on December
8, he declared that if the worst happened, he endorsed and called on
people to elect Nicolás Maduro as his successor who had been his
foreign minister for more than six years and had just been appointed
vice president.

During the months between the gubernatorial elections and the
Commander's death in March 2013, public confrontations within
the opposition surfaced. Perhaps the main point of controversy, or
the primary evidence, was that in the presidential elections, Chávez
had won in all the states of the country except for two—Táchira and
Mérida in the Andes—where the campaign responsibility lay with
AD and not with the "new" parties. The public and somewhat private
confrontation featured AD's Secretary General, Henry Ramos Allup,
attacking the *sifrinos* and anti-political parties, namely PJ and VP,
for their inability to engage in politics and for limiting themselves
to a discourse-driven diva-ism adequately promoted with financial
steroids on social media and television.

Ramos Allup had never hidden his disdain for the pretentious
champions of "new politics." On the other side, a disheartened and
diminished Capriles made efforts to be the spokesperson for the new
generation, continuously humiliated in public discussions. Thus, a
fracture began to operate within the main opposition parties, which
would later conventionally be referred to as the G4: AD and UNT
(ultimately a regional split but still social-democratic) against PJ and

VP. The first group defended realpolitik and the formal elements of the rules of the game, even if they did not agree with them. Meanwhile the other sector maintained a confrontational, spoiled, and rupturist vision. This rift would continue to widen.

The seismic death of the Commander signified a new call to arms. Now, said the opposition, this is the end, and we will reclaim what is ours. Once again, on April 14, 2013, Capriles faced off in elections against Chávez's chosen candidate, Maduro, and was defeated for the second consecutive time, although the margin between the two candidates was reduced compared to the elections of the previous October.

At that moment, with the official results announced, the first signs of what was to come became evident. By refusing to accept the results, a violent response was activated that once again brought the *guarimbas* back to the scene, as mobs began to storm and attack party headquarters, CNE offices, health centers of the Misión Barrio Adentro, and, where possible, residences of the Gran Misión Vivienda Venezuela, killing about fifteen people and injuring a hundred.

The main lines of destabilization were clear: disavowal, political destabilization, and economic warfare. In the following months, far from being tension-free, the third element expanded with boycotts, hoarding of goods, capital flight, and the exacerbation of the currency control regime. Still, by the end of the year, municipal elections were called, in which Capriles assumed the political and campaign leadership, turning the electoral confrontation into a "plebiscite." For the third time in less than a year, he was defeated, with Chavismo taking two-thirds of the 335 municipalities. Once again, the internal war between traditional sectors and anti-political elements was publicly visible, with the former once again reproaching the lack of will to engage in politics and for seeking arbitrary solutions, whatever they might be.

Curiously, the end of 2013, after some peaks of intensity, closed with a peculiar atmosphere of concord, in which beyond formal politics, there grew a unique climate of détente, forecasting a remote but potential possibility that channels of understanding could prevail over confrontation. President Maduro himself, after the elections, called for a national dialogue that included all recently elected mayors and opposition governors (excluding Capriles).

In that same meeting, the first signs began to emerge that such a path would not be possible.

THE YEARS OF WAR (2014-2022)

As the dividing line became clearer between the realist, traditional faction and the anti-political one, the strike occurred. La Salida (The Exit) was a violent operation led by Leopoldo López, María Corina Machado, and Antonio Ledezma, and would initiate the first major cycle of violence. The central thesis of their discourse was persistent: there are no legal or electoral mechanisms to "escape the regime," only the streets. "The world is on our side," they claimed.

La Salida, as someone undeniably from the opposition once told me, has been the darkest pact in Venezuelan politics. Much of what was unleashed on February 14, 2014, took most observers by surprise. Indeed, the consecutive defeats both in the streets and at the polls had created a brief period of détente (the true social reflection of the moment) and ruled out the possibility of such an assault, citing the opposition's lack of strength. This general atmosphere was more conducive to creating instances of agreement between antagonists. But this possibility of understanding was the worst imaginable scenario from the perspective of regime change laboratories outside our borders. And it has always been.

Just as the trend of division between the two major lines of opposition (identifiable at least since 2004) could be traced—between realpolitik and disruption—a complementary vector also emerged: during major junctures, factions unify (under US guidance) for that objective. Generally, it is the quick and destructive formulas that prevail. Unity of command is dictated from outside our borders.

La Salida marked the starting point of open war and became the symbol of the traumatic division of Venezuelan society (aspiring to what is irreconcilable between the parties, to incurable wounds, to a climate of civil war). The era of hybrid warfare began in full, according to the formula established by Andrew Korybko: unconventional warfare plus color revolutions.

The calculations in the (unbalanced) minds of a López or a Machado are one thing; the calculations of the circus owners are another. The psychopathic personalities leading the charge might believe they are spearheading the adventure that will lead them to the presidential seat, but the calculations within US power circles (regardless of the party or lobby to which the politicians owe their allegiance) aim to survey the entire battlefield. Thus, the latter, for one reason or another, will win: either the revolt succeeds, or if defeated, the resulting violence from the confrontation will become narrative raw material, the legal basis for establishing the sanctions regime, just as it has been done.

This is the same "pattern of aggression" (the concept comes from historian Kate Hudson) that unfolds in the geopolitical zones dissenting from the "rules-based order." In these major junctures, with unified criteria in methods, discussions about which line of action to take become less clear, and the desires almost entirely come from outside our borders. This externalization of command, methods, and decisions will characterize the decade of war in its successive iterations. The tactical modifications as time progresses will respond to the preestablished notions held by those managing the instances of formal (and covert) politics in Washington (be it the White House, Foggy Bottom, K Street, or the Treasury Department). The think tank (or not) that provides the roadmap and strategies may change, but the objective remains the same, transcending the Democrat-Republican binary.

The complete subordination to the managers of the "opposition unity," along with the disappearance of criticism toward anti-political tantrums, was evidenced by the electoral victory in the 2015 legislative elections. It was Ramos Allup, not another, who, seizing the unique opportunity to employ all his cunning and strictly political experience, outlined in his inaugural speech as the first president of the National Assembly the main goal of the legislature: to remove President Maduro within six months. While not explicitly stated, that assertion marked a significant rupture in maintaining a reserve of forms and "prestige" that his identity as a true politician had possessed; instead he turned toward the schizophrenic utopia of express regime change. Clearly, he saw a golden opportunity internally, likely reinforced by the situational "analysis" loop with the United States and the directive to unify all efforts in pursuit of the same goal.

For the next five years, the illusion of operational (and discursive) unity would become a constant, and Venezuela would suffer the greatest pressure and destructive effort at the hands of the opposition and the US. This would push the institutional system of the Venezuelan state to its maximum point of tension, without even considering the effects or collateral damage toward the people, or at least acknowledging the possibility that Nicolás Maduro's government would have anything at its disposal to defend itself.

Thus, for five years, Venezuela was subjected to a dramatic number of political, social, and economic engineering actions that sought, as María Corina Machado often says, the coveted "breaking point." In this context, no substantial fissures emerged at the top of the G4. Despite presenting the idea of regime change as a "Venezuelan" effort, each facet adopted by the main currents of the opposition (which now also included a leftist arm) depended entirely, almost exclusively, on the United States and its European colonies in tow.

The six years from 2014 to 2020 essentially opened the door to the most destructive and aggressive direct (and indirect) intervention in Venezuela's history, aside from the voluntary one that marked the country throughout much of the twentieth century.

As these kinds of schemes, dependent on gringos and genetically modified, are difficult to sustain, the cracks in the apparent consensus did not come from the center of the G4 party leadership but from its own periphery. As the "governmental" charade with Juan Guaidó at the helm deflated, members of parliament who were not part of the front line of PJ, AD, UNT, and other parties staged a parliamentary coup against Guaidó starting in 2020. Whether they were exemplary or not, this did not make them any less (1) representatives of their parties at the regional level, excluded from the overall process; and (2) politicians who, with nothing to show for their work by this point, except for the Guaidó charade, had understood that the fate of their careers would be even more buried than that of the main protagonists—they would be economically protected, secured, and sent to play banker, for example, at some third-rate university in South Florida.

Operation Gideon[1], the last resonant milestone of the Guaidó tragicomedy, caused even greater reputational damage to the supposed struggle for Venezuela's "freedom." This, in turn, deepened the

---

1   On May 3, 2020, a group of mercenaries, including two former US special forces, attempted to enter Venezuela on the coast of the La Guaira State to carry out assassinations of Venezuelan political leaders. They arrived in speed boats from Colombia and were captured by fishermen in La Guaira.

internal conflicts of leadership: the damage control process inevitably forced certain names into the spotlight.

In any case, this stage of the ongoing coup, in terms of facts, minimized any semblance of differential identity between the two major currents. Meanwhile the smaller internal factions that did not publicize their dissatisfaction or unease disregarded tradition and instead followed the most basic logic that has marked the path of the various right-wing opposition formations (along with the economic and business interests behind them): blatant, open intervention, without nuances and without calculating the consequences for both the country and for the essence of a nationally meaningful opposition.

These internal struggles, a product of the unacknowledged and unrecognized political defeat, also translated, on one hand, into the judicial intervention of parties like PJ and AD who were disputing who would assume the legitimate leadership of the coalitions. On the other hand, in the particular case of VP, leading each of these vitriolic events resulted in an implosion where practically the entire leadership fled the region, which included, among others, the unfortunate Juan Guaidó being deported from Colombia and "humanely" received in Florida.

Another aspect was the inevitable pragmatism that drove the parties to resume the dialogues sponsored by Norway and Mexico, establishing as a roadmap, two years later, what would become the Barbados Agreements, when UNT, primarily, decided to take a step back from the abyss.

We could speak of a sustained process of denationalization of these parties in relation to the Venezuelan population, whether sympathetic or not. Skepticism and rejection of everything associated with politics were further accentuated, and the people were already severely battered by the general degradation of life under the sanctions regime. A significant number of people who decided to embark on the path of emigration experienced the shock and tragedy of effectively becoming a migrant population when Venezuela had practically never been one. They encountered firsthand what it was like to live exposed to xenophobia, the fluctuations of globalization, and the deception that many politicians in the Lima Group[2] countries peddled as truth in 2017 and 2018. They were "invited" to Chile, Colombia, or Peru, but

---

2   A grouping of center and right-wing leaders in Latin America founded in Lima in 2017 in order to leverage regional diplomatic, political, and economic attacks against Venezuela.

their experience stood in stark contrast to the dolce vita of Leopoldo López in the north of Madrid.

When Joe Biden assumed the presidency in 2021, the maximum pressure campaign of the previous administration seemed to let up, yet it was still unclear what the Democratic administration would bring in its place (after all, the open war with Venezuela was inaugurated with Obama at the helm). In 2022, the new approach of the White House began to manifest ambiguously (as it has been thus far). Increasingly, Venezuela became less of an object of international attention, and Latin America, with new governments, gradually dismantled the remnants of the regional monstrosity that was assembled with the Lima Group.

On the other hand, the war in Ukraine forced the indecisive US government to engage in a direct exchange, an anemic yet existential rapprochement. Driven strictly by energy concerns and the effects of the sanctions imposed on Russia—similar to those imposed by Europe—the Biden administration looked toward Venezuela under the "humanitarian" pretext of addressing the various US citizens imprisoned for different reasons. The US took steps to attempt "normalization" and "dialogue," stripping all previous momentum from the various violent regime-change attempts despite never fully disavowing Guaidó as "interim president" until well into 2023 nor recognizing Maduro's legitimacy. These attempts never translated into abandoning efforts to expel Chavismo from power, instead focusing, or so they claimed, on an electoral exit and the activation of a transitional process (a key term referring to the liquidation of uncomfortable agents).

THE MARÍA CORINA CHAPTER (2023-2024)

Signs of economic recovery came with an internal impact. Since Venezuela's energy market and traditional oil partners were simply incurring losses, there was a nuanced granting of licenses to trade oil due to the pressure and lobbying of oil businesses like Chevron—primarily, but not exclusively. Without the force of extortionate pressure from the parties for a quick exit directly funded by the United States, the main national economic and financial groups began to publicly acknowledge the negative impact of sanctions on their interests, admitting that it was better business to work with the government to recover.

Here, a significant shift occurred. Fedecámaras, the main business association of the entrepreneurial groups, set aside its usual anti-Chavismo belligerence and joined the national economic consensus. Let's not forget that Pedro Carmona Estanga, known as "Carmona the Brief," was the "president" of the 2002 coup for forty-seven hours while also serving as the president of the Fedecámaras.

With the presidential elections of 2024 around the corner, once again, with a fair amount of lead in their wings, the opposition political parties set out to designate their "unitary" candidate through "primaries." As seen from late 2023 to the elections on July 28, 2024, this process was a co-opted, maneuvered, and manipulated process by the only ultra sector still standing that had not burned through almost all its political cartridges the previous decade: María Corina Machado and her party/NGO, Vente Venezuela.

The main brahmin of anti-politics was convinced that her time had come. With regards to other groups and figures in the anti-political sphere, even if there are no significant differences in substance, their differences in form manifest in how Machado has represented herself compared to the rest of the cast of characters and strategies. The most important difference lies in the fact that Machado has always positioned herself as the most radical, "risk-taking" version, who fears the least in naming things as they are.

In the face of attempts to downplay the elements that have highlighted the worldview and socioeconomic background of all the previous figures, Machado has never been shy about openly expressing, in no uncertain terms, the need for direct international intervention, the efficacy (and necessity) of sanctions, and being just a few steps away from proclaiming that the only solution regarding Chavismo is persecution, death, and eradication, all under the label of transition. Her hostility has not been limited to the government and Chavismo; she has also directed it toward the rest of the political establishment. In her eyes as a Brahmin, everyone else is Dalit. Moreover, they are cowards. While others in the opposition made a tremendous effort to show they had a people's face, that they all accepted the constitution, and even claimed that if they came to power, they would "improve" social missions (as Capriles often claimed in his first campaign), Machado promoted what she defined as "popular capitalism."

While most evaded or excessively relativized the role and effects of sanctions, hiding that they favored the option of direct military intervention, and in some cases publicly moderating their support for Guaidó, María Corina took pride in stating the fine print. Beyond the usual class arrogance, perhaps the rest of the explanation lies more in the psychiatric than in the political.

As if automatic, every international antagonist of the government deserved to be contacted and, where possible, to propose alliances or other expressions of unconditionality with the agenda. This included declaring herself a liberal in a nod to Javier Milei and announcing that if she won the elections, she would restore diplomatic relations with Israel by relocating the Venezuelan embassy to Jerusalem.

But it is impossible not to perceive the levels of pretense in anything proposed, in the ways she presents herself publicly, in her manner of speaking, and in the attitudes she has assumed in recent years toward the poor—whom she has always structurally despised but who are an indispensable piece in undermining support for Chavismo, especially alongside the economic effects of the blockade. Her electoral rise, despite having to carry it out "by proxy" in two exemplary cases of geriatric abuse, has followed a plan and a process of **radically synthetic ascent**, now evident after the elections of July 28. She has methodically occupied each of the positions that should grant her organicity and legitimacy in the internal contest of the Democratic Unitary Platform (PUD), the current avatar of the Coordinadora Democrática. Each conquered stage could, in turn, be interpreted as the emptying of substance from each position, reduced to the instrumentalization of the "greater agenda" and the preestablished structures to produce the necessary engineering of perception. Without underestimating her temperament (however psychopathic) and her unbearable consistency, one can see this to be the case: neither the analysis that organizes the dynamics of factors and variables, nor the methods to achieve the same old goal regarding the last twenty-five years in Venezuela are hers. In that same anxiety, arrogance, and impatience, it is impossible to find the capacity for complex analysis reflected in the guidelines and steps of this new edition of regime change.

In contrast to the gangster-like exit attempt of the Trump administration, the Democrats appealed to subsidiary forces, to an indirect and multi-stakeholder approach, believing that the solution was electoral. The main reference was the double defeat in the state of Barinas in 2021 and 2022, accompanied by a transitional process (a de-Baathification) overseen by experts from the NGO–industrial complex. Perhaps the public promoter of this line has been Marcela Escobari, first from her position as Assistant Administrator of the Caribbean and Latin America Bureau of USAID under Samantha Power, and now as the chief advisor on migration for the National Security Council. Without seeking to overstate Escobari's role without sufficient evidence, it is very difficult not to connect the dots between her two recent positions and the forces that have manifested in this new round of coup attempts—triggers capable of shaping both the streets and the informational landscape in networks and media.

With an opposition establishment devastated in its most radical manifestations as well as in the various approaches between sections of the G4 itself and the government (which for Machado are signs of capitulation and collaboration), the main forces left standing are organized crime for the former and the diaspora for the latter. If Escobari's role cannot be consistently accepted as rector, one can acknowledge that there is a generalized structural reflection of the conception of the possible plan against Venezuela.

Machado, unlike previous shipwrecked politicians, has had heavy and frontline coverage from 2023 to the present *(The Economist, Wall Street Journal, New York Times,* etc.), even more substantial than any predecessor. Her interaction with transatlantic politicians from all sides and the formation of her own team of notable figures drawn from Ivy League and Oxbridge schools magnifies the role of "the international" (the United States and Europe), almost reducing the role of the Venezuelan context to zero, except as an audience or a rowdy supporter. This marks the main differentiating factor from all previous schemes. It seems that no resources are being spared, perhaps due to the "guarantees" that María Corina offers as an unconditional ally, along with her little moral reflection on the harm involved in achieving goals "her" way.

Another element supporting the theory of a structural reflection above is the use of the Venezuelan diaspora, particularly encouraging younger sectors. Perhaps the most recent sociological phenomenon now established and less studied in the Venezuelan moment, her consideration and (ab)use of this demographic is hardly recognized as anyone else's merit. As the diaspora is clearly demarcated and segmented regarding class background, professional preparation, access to job markets, treatment based on context, and of course, status (once again, Brahmins and Dalits), Team Machado's campaign relies on those with a systematic and permanent online presence. They target those aligned with her worldview regarding what should be done with Venezuela and the Revolution, practically taking for granted which segment of the migration is mobilized and engages with the discourse.

Notably, while that same diaspora comprises a consolidated managerial class, or more importantly, is preparing and benefiting from the "opening" in academia, especially within the US university system (reaching sectors of the academic middle class), the influence of contemporary currents, whether libertarian or woke, is much more noticeable. Both operate, from their distinct semantic fields, to articulate the discourse that accompanies the upheaval.

A new "generation that knows what it's doing" builds, generally against the backdrop of life within Venezuela, its own disassociated concept of the homeland, a common sense of the times, along the same lines of continuity, only more exposed to the trends in vogue in the collective West.

Ultimately, and with a lack of ingenuity comparable to that which afflicts the United States, the tradition of anti-politics once again sets the agenda. While inhibiting (attacking or pressuring) more traditional political initiatives that have encompassed the vast and complicated spectrum of what could be opposition politics in Venezuela, the anti-political is like a disturbed platypus, a mishmash of different elements. Like all forms of struggle, it combines symbolic elements, the fashionable language, and the opportunistic and circumstantial imprint of methods. The discourse persists with a fixed objective, while conveniently denying its identification as right-wing according to its interests or as left-wing in its attempts to be digestible.

Nothing seems to escape the liberal matrix, regardless of where it stands on the horizontal axis, but this is a secondary matter, while the need to reclaim the organization of the vertical axis (the preservation of the above over the below) returns to its antecedent in the twentieth century.

❖❖❖❖❖

In particular, the first part of this work relied in a disorganized and indiscriminate manner on the writings of leftist thinkers from the twentieth century, such as Pedro Duno, Domingo Alberto Rangel, Alfredo Maneiro, and Kléber Ramírez, as well as chroniclers who, not from the left, have narrated the 1990s, like Juan Carlos Zapata, Mirtha Rivero, and Gloria Bastidas. In the era of Chavismo, it was composed of original research or teamwork conducted for over ten years from Misión Verdad.